A Parent's Guide to Living With Adult Children

Strategies to Master Boundaries and Communication to Avoid Conflict and Build Connection

Catherine Jennings

© **Copyright 2024 - All rights reserved.**

The content contained within this book may not be reproduced, duplicated or transmitted without direct written permission from the author or the publisher.

Under no circumstances will any blame or legal responsibility be held against the publisher, or author, for any damages, reparation, or monetary loss due to the information contained within this book, either directly or indirectly.

Legal Notice:

This book is copyright protected. It is only for personal use. You cannot amend, distribute, sell, use, quote or paraphrase any part, or the content within this book, without the consent of the author or publisher.

Disclaimer Notice:

Please note the information contained within this document is for educational and entertainment purposes only. All effort has been executed to present accurate, up to date, reliable, complete information. No warranties of any kind are declared or implied. Readers acknowledge that the author is not engaged in the rendering of legal, financial, medical or professional advice. The content within this book has been derived from various sources. Please consult a licensed professional before attempting any techniques outlined in this book.

By reading this document, the reader agrees that under no circumstances is the author responsible for any losses, direct or indirect, that are incurred as a result of the use of the information contained within this document, including, but not limited to, errors, omissions, or inaccuracies.

Table of Contents

THE BOOMERANG GENERATION 1

CHAPTER 1: BOUNDARIES: WHEN AN INCH BECOMES A MILE 5

    WHAT ARE BOUNDARIES AND WHY ARE THEY IMPORTANT? 6
    HOW TO SET UP GREAT BOUNDARIES 7
    THE TOUGH LOVE APPROACH: IS IT WORTH IT? 10
    A BALANCING ACT 12
    HOW TO RESPOND TO RESISTANCE 13

CHAPTER 2: NURTURING RELATIONSHIPS 17

    NAVIGATING THE SHIFT TO AN ADULT-ADULT RELATIONSHIP 18
        Challenges and Benefits 18
        Get Practical 19
    MASTERING THE ART OF RESPECTING PRIVACY 21
        Communicating Boundaries 21
    SUPPORTING WITHOUT ENABLING: OFFERING HELP THE RIGHT WAY 23
    MANAGING DIFFICULT CHANGES: ESTRANGEMENT AND DIVORCE 25
    REDEFINING ROLES: IS YOUR CHILD NOW YOUR CAREGIVER? 27
    RELATIONSHIP RESET: WIPING THE SLATE CLEAN 29
    LOVE IS LOVE: ACCEPTING YOUR ADULT CHILD'S LIFESTYLE CHOICES 31

CHAPTER 3: THE ART OF CO-EXISTING—SHARING SPACES, STRONGER BONDS 35

    FINDING BALANCE: NEGOTIATING PRIVACY AND AUTONOMY 36
    MASTERING CONFLICT RESOLUTION UNDER ONE ROOF 38
    DISCUSSING THE STRAIN ON RELATIONSHIPS 40
    BLENDED FAMILIES AND STEP-CHILDREN 42
    LIVING WITH GRANDCHILDREN: BRIDGING THE GENERATION GAP 45
    EXTENDING AN INVITATION TO CONNECT: MAKING OPPORTUNITIES FOR TOGETHERNESS 48

CHAPTER 4: EFFECTIVE COMMUNICATION—HOW TO CONNECT AND HAVE REAL CONVERSATIONS 51

    THE POWER OF ACTIVE LISTENING: WHEN "I HEAR YOU" ACTUALLY MEANS YOU'RE LISTENING 52
    SPEAKING WITHOUT CRITICISM 54
    USING "I" STATEMENTS: BECAUSE "YOU" STATEMENTS WON'T CUT IT 55
    CREATING SAFE SPACES FOR HONEST CONVERSATIONS 57

CHAPTER 5: PRACTICAL TIPS—PAYING THEIR WAY 59
- Paying Rent 60
- Shared Expenses and Utilities 63
  - Shared Resources: The Invisible Price Tag 63
  - Gradual Financial Responsibility: The Incremental Approach 64
  - Real Consequences: Economic Reality Check 64
- Addressing Financial Irresponsibility 65
- Retired Parents and Finances 67
- Encourage Saving and Financial Planning 68
  - Savings Accountability: The Balanced Contribution Model 69
- Dealing with Job Loss and Unemployment 71
  - Alternative Contributions: Sweat Equity Matters 71
  - Focus on Progress: Motivation Through Celebration 72
  - Support Their Search: Collaborative Empowerment 72
  - Balancing Financial Support With Self-Sufficiency: The Collaborative Contribution Model 73
  - Celebrate Growth: The Confidence Catalyst 74
- Neurodivergent Support: The Compassionate Adaptation Guide ... 74

CHAPTER 6: PRACTICAL TIPS—LIVING SPACES AND BUILDING THE HOME YOU WANT 77
- Discussing Household Goals 78
- Chores: Dividing and Conquering 79
- Managing Shared Spaces 81
  - Encouraging Time Management and Organization 82
- Dealing With Procrastination and Avoidance 84
- The Tough Love Approach: When "Pretty Please" Isn't Cutting It 85

CHAPTER 7: PRACTICAL TIPS—INTIMATE RELATIONSHIPS 87
- Respecting Everyone's Comfort Level 88
- Creating Space for Your Adult Child's Dating Life 89
  - Safety First 90
  - Boundaries and Communication 90
- Handling Breakups and Divorce 92
- My Adult Child Is LGBTQ+: Love Doesn't Need a Renovation Permit 94
- De-escalation Methods for Difficult Conversations 96

CHAPTER 8: PRACTICAL TIPS—POSITIVE MINDSET AND MENTAL WELLNESS 101
- The Elephant in Your Living Room: Mental Health Matters 102
- Narcissism 101 107
  - The Gaslighting Gambit: When Reality Becomes Optional 108
  - The Empathy Workout: Building Emotional Muscles 109

The Manipulation Playbook: Recognize and Deflect 110
THE VELCRO DILEMMA: ADDRESSING EMOTIONAL DEPENDENCE 111
Neurodivergence: The Brain's Scenic Route 113
SURVIVING THE EMOTIONAL THUNDERSTORM 114
THE NOCTURNAL NIGHTMARE: ENOUGH SLEEP 117
SUBSTANCE ABUSE: NAVIGATING THE MINEFIELD OF ADDICTION 119
The Warning Sign Decoder Ring 120
The Conversation 121
The Support Playbook 122

CHAPTER 9: SIMPLE BUT EFFECTIVE SELF-CARE HABITS FOR PARENTS............ 125

THE FREEDOM HEIST 126
The Freedom Wishlist: Reclaiming Your Emotional Real Estate 127
THE PROBLEM WITH KEEPING EVERYONE HAPPY 128
The Emotional Energy Bank 130
DEALING WITH GUILT 131
The Guilt Journal: Your Emotional Workout 132
ACCEPTING YOUR LIMITATIONS 134
The Jar of No: Your Boundary Collection 134
You're Not Perfect, and That's Okay! 136
WHO IS YOUR SUPPORT NETWORK? 138
Enjoy Your Retirement 139
SIMPLE SELF-CARE HABITS: BECAUSE YOU'RE WORTH IT 141
Self-Care Strategies 141

CONCLUSION: THE COUCH, THE CHAOS, AND THE UNEXPECTED GRACE OF PARENTING ADULT CHILDREN 145

REFERENCES 149

The Boomerang Generation

"Mom, Dad, I think I need to move back home."

Those eight words can send shockwaves through any empty nester's carefully curated peace. One minute you're debating whether to turn their bedroom into a meditation sanctuary, the next you're wondering if your retirement fund can survive another mouth to feed.

Welcome to the club nobody planned to join—parenting the boomerang generation.

Remember when you thought teaching them to ride a bike was hard? Try teaching them to "adult" while they're sprawled on your couch, streaming Netflix on your Wi-Fi, and eating the leftovers you were saving for tomorrow's lunch. According to recent statistics, you're in crowded company—52% of young adults now live with their parents, the highest percentage since the Great Depression (Fry et al., 2020). And no, that's not counting the ones who "temporarily" crash for "a few weeks" that mysteriously stretch into months.

"I raised them to be independent!" you protest, while simultaneously wondering if you should wake them for their noon job interview.

The truth? Of course, you did. But today's economic landscape looks more like a maze than a ladder. Sky-high rents, student loans that could fund a small country, and a job market that demands five years of experience for entry-level positions—it's enough to send anyone scurrying back to their childhood bedroom. This isn't a parenting failure. It's a societal shift that's left both generations scrambling for the instruction manual. Your adult child isn't the only one who needs guidance—you're on foreign territory too!

Are you their parent, their landlord, or their roommate? Hey, sometimes you're all three before breakfast.

The challenges stack up faster than their unwashed dishes. There's the financial strain—suddenly your grocery bill doubles while your savings shrink. Physical space becomes a premium commodity, with privacy becoming as rare as a millennial with a pension plan. You struggle to respect their autonomy while fighting the urge to remind them to wear a jacket when it's cold. Their mental health becomes your mental health, their anxiety fueling your insomnia. And don't get started on their dating life—though you certainly hear enough of it through those thin walls. Your relationship with your spouse might feel the strain too. One of you wants to set strict rules; the other's sneaking them gas money. You debate in whispered tones about enabling versus supporting, about tough love versus compassion. Meanwhile, your adult child alternates between treating you like their personal ATM and bristling at any suggestion that maybe, possibly, they could contribute to the household beyond their sparkling personality.

But here's the plot twist—this situation holds unprecedented opportunities for growth, connection, and yes, even joy. This book isn't another finger-wagging lecture about millennials and their avocado toast addiction. It's a practical roadmap for transforming potential family chaos into genuine adult relationships.

You'll discover how to:

- Navigate the parent-peer paradox without losing your mind
- Set boundaries that stick without triggering World War III
- Transform entitled behavior into mutual respect
- Preserve your marriage while managing your new houseguest
- Support without enabling
- Build authentic adult relationships with your children
- Maintain your own life and dreams while helping them achieve theirs

You'll learn why traditional parenting tactics backfire spectacularly with adult children, and how to develop new strategies that actually work.

We'll explore communication techniques that prevent eye-rolling (from both generations), and practical tips for everything from financial arrangements to bathroom schedules.

As someone who's spent years counseling families, I've seen every variation of this situation imaginable. I've witnessed the tears, celebrated the breakthroughs, and helped families forge stronger bonds through what initially felt like failure. This book exists because every parent deserves to know they're not alone. Your frustrations are valid. Your concerns are legitimate. Your hope for your child's success is admirable. But your own well-being matters too. Whether your adult child moved back yesterday or has been camping in your basement for years, whether they're actively job hunting or permanently glued to their gaming chair, whether they're dealing with mental health challenges or simply saving for their own place—this guide meets you where you are.

The boomerang generation represents a social phenomenon nobody prepared us for. But with the right tools, understanding, and support, it can become more than a crisis to endure. It can transform into an opportunity to know your children as adults, redefine family dynamics, and create relationships that enrich rather than drain. Ready to turn your home from a battlefield into a launching pad? Well, best you keep reading then. Because while nobody plans for their fledglings to return to the nest, we can certainly plan for their eventual, successful flight.

After all, parenting adult children is like making a soufflé—timing is everything, too much heat makes things collapse, and sometimes you need to read the recipe multiple times before getting it right.

Chapter 1:

Boundaries: When an Inch Becomes a Mile

One minute you're mastering the art of grocery shopping for two, the next you're wondering how one human can consume an entire week's worth of snacks in 48 hours.

It's the modern family remix. Between skyrocketing rents, student loans that look like phone numbers, and a job market that demands Olympic-level competition for entry-level positions, your spare room might be the most practical landing pad. But how do you parent an adult who doesn't want to be parented, support without enabling, and maintain your sanity while sharing space with someone who thinks midnight is a reasonable time to start cooking?

This chapter is all about the delicate dance of housing an adult child without losing your mind—or your retirement savings. We'll explore everything from setting boundaries that stick to managing expectations (both theirs and yours).

Because while your nest might not be empty anymore, it doesn't have to feel like a pressure cooker either.

What Are Boundaries and Why Are They Important?

Ah, when an inch becomes a mile. And that's exactly why boundaries exist—those invisible force fields that preserve sanity, protect resources, and let both generations maintain a healthy sense of identity.

But when adult children come knocking, boundaries can feel as fluid as a puddle on a hot summer day. One moment, there's joy in offering a safe haven where they can regroup; the next, you're frantically rearranging the fridge to fit an entire adult's appetite for homemade marinara. It's a balancing act. Give too much, and you might end up supporting a lifestyle of permanent adolescence. Give too little, and there's the risk of alienating them at a time when they need you most.

Without clear boundaries, that inch quickly becomes a mile. But it's rarely straightforward, especially with neurological differences in the picture. Take autism or ADHD, for instance. For individuals with these traits, boundaries can be tricky to navigate. Their brains process social cues and personal space differently, so what feels like a small request to you may seem overwhelming to them. That's where the challenge lies: finding a balance that respects their needs while preserving your own. It takes patience, creativity, and a lot of empathy to find common ground.

In the end, boundaries aren't about control or restriction. They're about creating a nurturing environment where everyone can thrive, respect each other's needs, and coexist harmoniously. Once you get the hang of it, boundaries start to feel less like rigid rules and more like a warm, comforting embrace.

So, where's the sweet spot? How do you set boundaries that protect your well-being while still nurturing their growth and independence?

How to Set Up Great Boundaries

When it comes to setting boundaries with adult children, there's no one-size-fits-all approach. These aren't little kids anymore—these are fully grown individuals with their own ideas, opinions, and often, stubborn ways of doing things. The days of simply "laying down the law" and expecting them to fall in line? That approach now works about as well as teaching a cat to tango.

Here's the thing: Trying to enforce rules often has a counterproductive effect. Instead of fostering cooperation, it can trigger the exact opposite—adult children digging in their heels, rebelling against what feels like an infringement on their independence. And who can blame them? After years of following our lead, they're naturally craving the freedom to make their own choices, even if it means we don't always agree with those choices. That's why successful boundary-setting with adult children requires collaboration. It's about sitting down together, hashing out expectations, and crafting an understanding that feels respectful and balanced. When they feel listened to and involved, they're much more likely to respect the boundaries you both establish.

Being clear, direct, and consistent is essential. You can't just drop vague hints about chores, financial contributions, or the need for personal space and expect them to read your mind. Lay everything out in black and white, and once these agreements are set, hold firm. Model the behavior you want to see, and be consistent in your communications. And yes, they might push back. That's when having a bit of backbone comes in handy. As much as we'd all love to be the "cool" parent, sometimes we have to say no and stick to it—whether it's about financial help, last-minute plans, or household routines. By doing so, you're equipping them with valuable skills for adulthood, like respecting boundaries and managing responsibility. How can they learn these skills if we're always swooping in to clean up every mess?

So, take a deep breath and get ready to put those boundary-setting skills to work. It may feel awkward at first, but with practice, it gets easier. And soon enough, those boundaries will solidify, letting you and your adult child coexist in a healthier, more harmonious way.

Setting and Maintaining Healthy Boundaries With Adult Children

1. **Identify your own needs and limits**

    o Start by understanding what you need to feel respected and maintain your well-being.

    o Identify specific areas where boundaries are essential (financial support, household rules, personal space).

2. **Define clear expectations**

    o Be specific about what behaviors you expect and where the boundaries lie. For example, if contributing to household chores or respecting curfews is important, make this explicitly clear.

    o Outline financial boundaries if applicable, such as limitations on borrowing money or expectations regarding rent.

3. **Have an open and respectful discussion**

    o Sit down with your adult child and have a direct, open conversation.

    o Frame the discussion as collaborative; ask for their thoughts and feelings on these boundaries to help them feel involved.

4. **Set boundaries together**

    o If they feel included in the decision-making process, they may be more likely to respect the boundaries.

    o Agree on key points together, which fosters mutual respect and understanding.

5. **Communicate boundaries clearly**
    - Once boundaries are established, communicate them in straightforward terms.
    - Avoid being vague; state things in a way that leaves little room for misinterpretation.

6. **Model the behavior you expect**
    - Demonstrate respect for your own boundaries by adhering to them consistently.
    - Avoid bending the rules you've set, as this can create confusion and make boundaries harder to enforce.

7. **Hold firm with consistency**
    - Stick to the agreed-upon boundaries, even when it's uncomfortable. If your adult child pushes back, gently remind them of your prior agreement.
    - Consistency reinforces the importance of the boundaries and helps prevent them from becoming fluid over time.

8. **Acknowledge and address resistance calmly**
    - If your adult child challenges the boundaries, stay calm and stick to the facts.
    - Use "I" statements, such as "I feel that my personal space is important" rather than "You're invading my space."

9. **Evaluate and adjust as needed**
    - Revisit boundaries periodically to see if adjustments are needed.

- Life changes, such as new jobs or moving out, may mean some boundaries need to be revised.

Tip: For troubled young adults struggling with issues like mental health challenges, addiction, or other life obstacles, approach boundaries with compassion but maintain structure:

- **Seek support**: Consider involving a therapist or counselor who can help mediate and offer strategies for both parties.

- **Provide resources, not solutions**: Encourage them to use available resources, such as support groups or job counseling, rather than stepping in to solve their problems.

- **Focus on stability**: Set boundaries that focus on creating stability, like requiring adherence to curfews, limiting financial support, or setting expectations for behavior in the household.

Setting boundaries in these cases requires patience and a balance between support and firmness to foster a positive environment while respecting your own limits.

The Tough Love Approach: Is It Worth It?

Ah, the temptation of tough love—that siren song whispering, "If you just stop enabling them, they'll finally get their act together!"

As a parent of the boomerang generation, you've probably flirted with the idea at one point or another. After all, why coddle adult children when a little good old-fashioned hardship might be just the kick in the pants they need? But before going full-on drill sergeant on your beloved returns, it's important to weigh the pros and cons of this approach. On the plus side, tough love can be a powerful motivator, forcing adult children to take responsibility for their own lives and stop relying on you as a crutch. If you stop bailing them out of every sticky situation, the thinking goes, they'll have no choice but to learn to "adult" on their own. And hey, maybe that means they'll finally get serious about finding a job, managing finances, or tackling that mountain of student debt.

However, the downside of this strategy is that it can also backfire spectacularly, leaving both generations feeling frustrated, resentful, and more estranged than ever. You see, the tough love approach is a bit like walking a tightrope—if you don't strike the perfect balance, you risk pushing your kids away just when they need you most. And let's not forget the emotional toll it can take on you as a parent—watching your child struggle without being able to step in and help? It's enough to make even the steeliest of parents crumble. So, what's really driving you to reach for the tough love playbook in the first place? Is it truly a last resort, a desperate attempt to kickstart your adult child's journey to independence? Or could it be that, deep down, you're actually trying to ease your own feelings of guilt and inadequacy?

As a parent, you're hardwired to want the best for your child—and when they're floundering, it's only natural to question whether you've failed them somehow. The truth is, as with plenty of parenting tips and advice, there's no one-size-fits-all answer when it comes to tough love. For some families, it may be the wake-up call their boomerang desperately needs to get their life on track. But for others, it could irreparably damage the delicate parent-child bond you've worked so hard to nurture. It's a high-stakes gamble and one that requires a clear-eyed assessment of your individual circumstances and the unique needs of your adult child. Perhaps the wisest approach is to view tough love as a tool in your parenting toolbox, rather than a one-size-fits-all solution. You can keep it in your back pocket, ready to deploy if all other attempts at boundary-setting and collaborative problem-solving have failed. But you should also be willing to put it aside if you sense that it's doing more harm than good—because at the end of the day, your primary goal should be to support your child's growth and independence, not to prove a point.

After all, this journey you're on together is uncharted territory for both generations. There's no perfect road map, no instruction manual that can tell you exactly what to do. But with a healthy dose of empathy, flexibility, and a willingness to adapt as you go, you can navigate these tricky waters and emerge stronger, wiser, and more closely bonded than ever before.

A Balancing Act

On one side, your nurturing, protective instincts scream to swoop in and "fix" every problem your adult child encounters. On the other, you know that true growth and independence can only come from letting them navigate their own path—even if it means watching them stumble now and then.

It's a delicate balance and one that requires a hefty dose of self-awareness, empathy, and the willingness to sometimes bite your tongue until it practically hurts.

The urge to dole out unsolicited advice is mighty strong. After all, you've been there, and you know a thing or two about the trials of adulting. But, truthfully, those words of "wisdom" rarely hit with the intended impact. Your adult children often hear them as thinly veiled criticism or as a sign that they're not quite measuring up. Instead, try to approach these conversations with an open mind and a genuine desire to understand. Resist the urge to jump in and "fix" things, and instead listen—really listen—to their struggles, aspirations, and the reasoning behind their choices. Sure, it may not align perfectly with your vision of success, but who's to say what's right for them? Then, there's the delicate dance of support versus enabling. It's a fine line between being the caring, nurturing parent they need and the crutch that ultimately holds them back. No amount of hand-holding or financial bailouts is going to teach them the invaluable lessons of responsibility, resilience, and self-reliance. In fact, it might do the opposite in the long run.

How can you tell if you've crossed into "enabler territory"?

One sign is the dreaded sense of entitlement—where your adult child seems to feel they deserve to have their every need met without putting in the work. It's a slippery slope, one that can erode their sense of self-worth and agency. Take a long, hard look in the mirror and honestly assess your own behavior. Are you inadvertently perpetuating an entitled mindset by shielding them from natural consequences? Are you so eager to relieve their discomfort that you're robbing them of chances to problem-solve and grow?

This isn't easy to confront. After all, you're wired to protect them and ensure their well-being. But sometimes, the most loving thing you can do is to step back, let them stumble, and trust that they have the strength to pick themselves up and keep moving forward. Because here's the thing—true growth, the kind that lasts, can only come from within. It's the product of facing challenges head-on, learning from mistakes, and building resilience and self-reliance. As much as you'd love to, you can't do that work for them. All you can do is provide a soft place to land, offer a listening ear, and gently guide them toward the tools and resources they need to succeed.

With patience, empathy, and a whole lot of faith in your beloved boomerang, you can strike that elusive balance—supporting without smothering, nurturing without enabling. And who knows? You might even learn a thing or two about resilience and growth along the way.

How to Respond to Resistance

"But I'm an adult!" they declare while leaving wet towels on your freshly vacuumed carpet. Of course, you want to scream, "Then act like one!" But setting boundaries with adult children requires more finesse than your old "because I said so" strategy.

Are those boundaries you're trying to establish actually doable, or are you secretly writing a wish list for the perfect roommate? Before you post that color-coded chore chart (that no one will read), ask yourself: Would you have met these expectations at their age? Remember that time you lived on ramen and considered pizza a food group? Setting realistic expectations isn't about lowering your standards—it's about creating a foundation that won't crack under pressure. Instead of demanding they transform into Martha Stewart overnight, start with the basics:

- A heads-up when they'll miss dinner

- Basic household contributions (yes, picking up those wet towels counts)

- Regular check-ins about their progress toward independence
- Financial transparency if you're supporting them

Now, about that disappointment that creeps in when they miss the mark (again). You imagined them launching into adulthood like an eagle soaring majestically toward success. Instead, they're more like a penguin waddling toward independence—endearing but not quite what you pictured. It's easy to expect big changes quickly, but young adults often need time (and a few mistakes) to grow into their responsibilities. Their timeline isn't your timeline. While your friend's daughter might be crushing it at her law firm, your son might still be figuring out which end of the laundry detergent pod goes in first. That's okay. Different runways, different takeoff speeds. Think of disappointment as your parental GPS recalculating. No, they're not taking the route you mapped out—they're meandering through the backroads of adulthood, occasionally hitting potholes you warned them about. But remember when you thought that pyramid scheme in '92 was your ticket to early retirement? Different decade, different mishaps. Their path might look more like a scavenger hunt than your carefully plotted career highway, and that's okay.

But here's the golden ticket question: Where's your limit? You need to draw a line between supporting and enabling faster than your adult child can say, "Can you spot me twenty bucks?"

Consider these non-negotiables:

- Respect for your home and belongings
- Basic communication about comings and goings
- Contribution to household expenses (even if minimal)
- Progress toward their goals (however small)
- No illegal activities under your roof
- Adherence to agreed-upon house rules

What won't you tolerate? Write it down. Put it somewhere visible. Maybe next to that fancy coffee maker everyone keeps using.

The key takeaway? You're not running a hotel, but you're not running a boot camp either. Finding the sweet spot between support and independence is like trying to fold a fitted sheet—nobody gets it perfect, but we keep trying. Here's your pep talk (no participation trophy included): You're doing better than you think. That knot in your stomach when they miss another job interview? That's not failure—that's love with boundaries trying to find its footing. Your adult child's resistance isn't personal; it's part of their growth process, like those awkward teenage years but with better hygiene (hopefully).

Keep this in mind: Every time you enforce a boundary, you're not being mean—you're being a mentor. Every time you resist the urge to solve their problems, you're teaching resilience. Every time you let them face the consequences of their choices, you're investing in their future.

You've got this. Even if "this" means reminding them for the thousandth time that dishes don't magically transport themselves to the dishwasher. Your boundaries aren't prison walls—they're the foundation of their future independence.

Tomorrow's another day. Another chance to balance love with limits. Another opportunity to show them what adult responsibility looks like.

Chapter 2:

Nurturing Relationships

Remember when your biggest parenting challenge was deciding if eating Play-Doh warranted a time-out? Those were the simple days. Now you're watching your fully-grown offspring attempt to adult while living under your roof, and that Play-Doh incident feels like amateur hour.

This is the grand transformation of Parenthood 2.0, where your role takes a significant shift. One moment you're biting your tongue as they explain cryptocurrency to you (because apparently, you "wouldn't understand"), and the next you're pretending not to notice they still can't operate the washing machine without FaceTiming you. This is the delicate art of loving your adult child even when their choices make you do a double take and doubt your parenting skills. Gone are the days of "Because I said so."

You're graduating from the school of parent-child dynamics to something far trickier: adult-to-adult relationships. Think of it as updating your parenting software—except this time, your child thinks they're the IT department.

But here's the beautiful mess of it all: Your relationship is evolving into something richer than you imagined. Sure, they might roll their eyes at your Facebook posts and cringe when you attempt their slang, but between the chaos of cohabitation and the comedy of cross-generational living, there's magic happening. You're becoming more than parents—you're becoming allies, friends. It's about learning to love the adults they are, not the adults you planned for them to be.

So let's look into this new landscape of love, where boundaries meet belonging.

Navigating the Shift to an Adult-Adult Relationship

Ah, the simple joys of early childhood—a time when your word was law and you were the undisputed captain of the family starship.

Those days have sailed off into the sunset, welcoming the brave new world of adult-child relationships! One moment you're the benevolent dictator, the next you're struggling to have your voice heard over the whir of their TikTok-fueled ambitions. This transition from parent-child to adult-adult is no small feat. It requires a complete rewiring of your parental mindset, one that trades absolute authority for the more nuanced dance of mutual respect. After all, those days of "Because I said so" have given way to a new era where your adult child's opinion carries just as much weight as your own.

Make no mistake, this shift can be equal parts exhilarating and excruciating. On one hand, you've finally reached that milestone of raising an independent thinker, someone who can (mostly) navigate the complexities of the "real world" without your constant intervention. But on the other, letting go of that familiar role of benevolent dictator can feel like you're untying your own lifeline.

Challenges and Benefits

This new dynamic is a delicate balancing act. You want to respect their autonomy, but part of you still yearns to offer unsolicited advice. You crave the deep, meaningful conversations you once had, but find yourself constantly biting your tongue, fearful of sounding overbearing or undermining their newfound agency. Let's weigh up some of these challenges and benefits:

Challenges	Benefits
Loss of control: Parents must let go of the familiar role as the primary decision-maker and authority figure.	**More mature relationship**: Transitioning to an adult-adult dynamic allows for a deeper, more fulfilling partnership based on mutual respect.
Emotional growing pains: Adjusting to the shift in power dynamics can be unsettling and trigger feelings of uncertainty or even grief.	**Increased understanding**: Letting go of the parent-child concept enables parents and adult children to truly know each other as individuals.
Differing expectations: Adult children may have different views on appropriate levels of involvement and decision-making.	**Strengthened bond**: When navigated successfully, this shift can bring the two generations closer together.

Get Practical

Let's look at some practical examples and tips on how you can make this transition as smoothly as possible:

- **Decision-making:** A parent's opinion is no longer automatically the final say. Discussions become collaborative, with both parties voicing their perspectives and compromising.
    - **Example:** When choosing a career path, the adult child's choice carries equal weight, even if it differs from the parent's preference.
- **Advice-giving:** Parents must learn to offer suggestions tactfully, rather than lecturing. Adult children are more receptive to input when they feel heard and respected.

- o **Example:** Instead of demanding an adult child clean their room, a parent might say, "I've noticed the room is asking for a bit of a clean-up. Would you need a hand with that?"

- **Financial matters:** Accountability and transparency become key as parents transition from being the sole providers to financial partners.

  - o **Example:** Discuss budgets, expenses, and savings goals openly, rather than parents unilaterally deciding how money is managed.

Tips

- Understand that the parent-child relationship was built on care, protection, and guidance during the child's formative years.

- Acknowledge that this dynamic must now evolve into a relationship based on equality and mutual respect as the child becomes an adult.

- Empower your adult child to make their own choices, even if they differ from your preferences.

- Offer support and advice only when asked, rather than imposing your opinions.

- Allow your child to take the lead and learn from their own experiences, successes, and mistakes.

- Recognize that transitioning to an adult-adult relationship takes time and may involve emotional "growing pains" for both you and your child.

- Be patient with yourself and your child as you navigate this new dynamic. Falling back into old parent-child patterns is normal.

- Communicate openly about the challenges you both face and work together to find a new balance that respects each other's autonomy.

Mastering the Art of Respecting Privacy

Remember when your child's bedroom was an open book, filled with the remnants of childhood dreams and the occasional pair of questionable socks? But now, as your once-dependent offspring transform into self-sufficient adults, the very spaces you once roamed freely have become guarded fortresses—bastions of privacy that require delicate navigation.

It's a tricky transition, this shift from unfettered access to carefully curated boundaries. After all, you're hardwired to want to know every detail of your child's life, to offer unsolicited advice, and to swoop in at the first sign of trouble.

But as your adult child spreads their wings and carves out their own identity, you must learn to respect their need for independence, emotional and otherwise. Privacy is essential for their personal growth and the development of a truly equal, adult-to-adult relationship. Overstepping these boundaries can lead to resentment, conflict, and the dreaded "You're just being nosy!" accusations. It's a delicate dance where missteps can jeopardize the very bond you hold most dear.

So, how do you strike the right balance?

Communicating Boundaries

Well, I have one word for you: communication. It starts with open and honest communication about the boundaries you both need to feel respected and secure. By laying your cards on the table, you establish a safe space where both you and your child can express your needs, worries, and limits without fear of judgment.

If you dance around the topic or avoid tough conversations, you risk building up resentment and confusion. Clear is kind; being wishy-washy is not.

- Sharing your own need for privacy normalizes the concept for both of you—you model that it's not just a "rule" but a shared value that applies to everyone. This honesty fosters equality. As a parent, you must be clear about your own privacy concerns—whether it's respecting the sanctity of your bedroom or maintaining the illusion that you don't actually live in a constant state of unpacked boxes.
    - **Avoid:** Boundaries are about respect, not punishment or control, so avoid making it one-sided or using privacy as a way to get back at them.
- At the same time, you must encourage your adult child to voice their needs, creating an environment of mutual understanding. This approach builds their confidence in setting boundaries and empowers them to advocate for themselves. After all, what feels like a small request to you may seem overwhelming to them, especially if they process social cues and personal space differently due to neurological differences like autism or ADHD. Recognizing that everyone has different comfort levels and processing styles helps create a genuinely inclusive environment.
    - **Avoid:** Don't interrupt, dismiss, or label their concerns as "quirks" or "phases," even if you don't understand or agree with them. Underestimating the importance of their preferences, especially if rooted in neurodiversity, can make them feel misunderstood and dismissed.
- It's a give-and-take dance. Approach it with empathy, flexibility, and a genuine desire to cultivate trust. Those closed doors aren't barriers at all—they're gateways to deeper, more meaningful connections. Trust is the reward for this approach.

- **Avoid:** Don't treat boundaries as rigid rules or tests. While consistency is important, overly strict or "my way or the highway" stances can shut down any chance for compromise, making your child feel controlled rather than understood.

At the end of the day, respecting privacy is about building bridges. It's about honoring each other's autonomy while strengthening the bond that transcends the parent-child divide.

Supporting Without Enabling: Offering Help the Right Way

Remember that moment when your toddler insisted on tying their own shoes? You watched them fumble with those laces, knowing you could do it in seconds. But you waited because that's how they learned.

Fast-forward twenty years, and here you are, fighting that same instinct to swoop in and fix everything.

"Mom, I'm broke again..." Those words can twist your heart faster than a midnight phone call. Your hand's already reaching for your wallet before they finish the sentence. After all, isn't that what parents do? Not so fast.

Supporting your adult child while avoiding the enabling trap is like walking a tightrope in stilettos—tricky but not impossible. The difference? Support builds bridges to independence; enabling constructs walls around growth. When you're constantly playing financial firefighter or job-search guru, you're not helping them develop their own problem-solving muscles.

Let's say your daughter's facing eviction because she spent rent money on concert tickets. The enabling parent writes a check. The supporting parent helps her brainstorm solutions—maybe picking up extra shifts or selling unused items. One approach teaches responsibility; the other teaches that Mom and Dad's wallet is Plan A.

Here's what healthy support looks like:

- Being an emotional sounding board without solving their problems
- Offering advice only when they ask (yes, bite your tongue!)
- Celebrating their successes, no matter how small
- Standing back while they figure things out, even when it's painful to watch

And here's what enabling looks like:

- Repeatedly bailing them out of financial messes
- Making excuses for their behavior
- Taking responsibility for their obligations
- Solving problems that they should handle themselves

Setting boundaries in this regard isn't being mean—it's being wise. Maybe you'll help with unexpected medical bills but not credit card debt. Or you'll provide temporary housing but expect job-hunting progress reports. Whatever your limits, communicate them clearly and stick to them.

Think of support as giving them a flashlight in the dark, not carrying them through it. They might stumble, they might take wrong turns, but that's how they'll learn to find their way. And isn't that what we wanted all along? Adults who can stand on their own two feet, even if they wobble sometimes?

Your role isn't to prevent all pain—it's to be there when they need someone to talk to, encourage them when they're ready to try again, and believe in them even when they don't believe in themselves. That's not enabling; that's empowering.

Managing Difficult Changes: Estrangement and Divorce

Sometimes life throws curveballs that make teaching them to drive look like a walk in the park. Your adult child's marriage crumbles, or worse, they stop returning your calls altogether.

The parenting "manuals" never covered this chapter, did they?

Let's tackle the elephant in the living room first: estrangement. One day you're sharing Sunday dinners, the next you're analyzing their social media posts like a detective piecing together a mystery. The silence between calls grows longer, the responses shorter, until communication dims to birthday cards and occasional texts. "Give them space," well-meaning friends advise, while you fight every maternal instinct screaming to fix it. But here's the uncomfortable truth: Sometimes space is exactly what they need. Love doesn't vanish in silence—it waits patiently in the wings, ready when they are.

For those facing estrangement, here's your survival guide:

- Keep the door open without camping in the doorway
- Send occasional messages of love without demanding responses
- Focus on healing yourself; you can't pour from an empty cup
- Seek support from others who understand
- Always remember: this chapter isn't necessarily the end of the story

Then there's divorce. Your child's world implodes, and suddenly they're sleeping in their old bedroom again, surrounded by high school trophies while their own marriage trophy lies shattered. You want to unleash your mama bear rage on their ex, but pause. Your role isn't to lead the charge but to provide a safe harbor in the storm.

Supporting a divorcing adult child requires a very healthy dose of finesse:

- Be their emotional support without fueling the fire
- Listen without judgment (yes, even when they made questionable choices)
- Resist the urge to play lawyer/therapist/private investigator
- Keep the grandkids out of the crossfire
- Hold your tongue about their ex (they might reconcile!)

Whether dealing with divorce or estrangement, your adult child needs to know three things:

- you're there
- you love them
- you trust them to handle their own life

Sometimes that means watching from the sidelines while they rebuild their world. Other times it means being their temporary shelter while they find their feet.

The hardest part is to accept that you can't fix everything anymore. But you can be there, steady as a lighthouse, offering guidance without controlling the ship's course. And sometimes, that's exactly what they need—not a rescuer, but a beacon showing them they're not alone in the dark.

These challenges test relationships like steel in fire. They might bend, but with patience, understanding, and unconditional love, they don't have to break.

Redefining Roles: Is Your Child Now Your Caregiver?

Life has a funny way of coming full circle, doesn't it? One minute you're packing their lunch, the next they're helping you button your coat. That role reversal hits hard and twice as unexpectedly.

The same child who once rebelled against your rules about bedtime is now setting gentle but firm boundaries about your independence. "Dad, maybe it's time to consider a walking cane," they suggest, and suddenly you're transported back to that moment you first suggested they use training wheels. The roles have shifted, but the love behind the concern remains unchanged.

This new chapter brings its own cocktail of emotions:

- Pride in seeing your child step up with such competence
- Frustration at losing bits of independence
- Gratitude for their support
- Resistance to being "parented" by your own child

The secret? Maintaining dignity isn't about refusing help—it's about accepting it gracefully while holding onto your sense of self. You're still the parent who taught them compassion by example. Now they're showing you they learned those lessons well.

Consider these strategies for this delicate dance:

- Keep making decisions about your life whenever possible.
    - **Think:** "I'd love your input, but I think I'm going to go with my original plan for now."

- Share your wisdom and experience (they still need it!).
    - **Think:** "I went through something similar when I was your age. If you're interested, I can share what helped me."
- Accept help for tasks that have become challenging.
    - **Think:** "Sure, I'd be grateful if you could give me a hand with this—it's getting a bit harder for me these days."
- Maintain separate interests and social connections.
    - **Think:** "I'm actually heading out to a book club meeting tonight. Let's catch up tomorrow and I'll tell you about it!"
- Communicate openly about your needs and boundaries.
    - **Think:** "I really appreciate everything you do, but I still need some time to myself to mull things over. Let's find a balance that works for both of us."

Think of it as co-piloting rather than handing over the controls entirely. You're still an active participant in the route planning.

Accepting care from your adult child doesn't diminish your role as their parent. It simply adds new dimensions to your relationship. The story keeps getting richer, even as the characters evolve. Isn't this what you prepared them for? To be capable, caring adults who can handle life's challenges with grace?

Maybe this phase isn't about role reversal at all. Perhaps it's about roles expanding without erasing what came before.

Relationship Reset: Wiping the Slate Clean

Just think of those old VHS tapes you used to record over—sometimes the best way forward is to press that reset button and start fresh.

Your relationship with your adult child might need the same little pause and reset. No, I'm not saying erase the past (that's unrealistic and impossible). But you can choose to record new memories over old patterns. Remember when they'd slam their bedroom door, and you'd count to ten before knocking? Now they might be ghosting your texts, and you're still counting—except it's days between responses. Those old parenting moves that worked when they were fifteen? About as effective now as a flip phone at a youth convention.

"But that's how we've always done things!" you protest. Well, your daughter also used to think boy bands were the height of musical genius, and your son considered pizza rolls a food group. Things change. People grow. Relationships need to keep up.

Here's what a relationship reset looks like:

- Acknowledging that yesterday's solutions might be today's problems
    - **Why:** By letting go of the past "fixes," you're showing flexibility, a crucial ingredient for a strong adult-to-adult bond.
- Letting go of the "parent knows best" script
    - **Why:** Trusting their decisions lets them know you see them as capable adults.
- Trading lectures for conversations
    - **Why:** Conversations invite connection and respect, whereas lectures can feel patronizing. It's about mutual respect, rather than hierarchy.

- Replacing judgment with curiosity
    - **Why:** Approaching their choices with curiosity rather than judgment shows that you're interested in understanding their world, not controlling it.
- Understanding that forgiveness goes both ways
    - **Why:** Recognizing that both of you have grown, stumbled, and evolved fosters compassion and lets you both focus on moving forward.

The magic happens when both sides lay down their well-worn battle armor. Maybe you stop bringing up that time they dropped out of college, and they stop reminding you about the missed dance recital of '02. It's not about pretending these things never happened—it's about choosing not to let them define your tomorrow.

Consider having "the talk"—not that awkward birds-and-bees conversation from their teens, but an honest discussion about where you both want this relationship to go. Imagine it like redecorating a room together: What stays? What goes? What new elements would make this space more comfortable for everyone? The reset button is about creating space for new possibilities. It's a relationship renovation rather than a demolition. You're not tearing down the foundation of love and shared memories; you're adding modern amenities like mutual respect, adult-to-adult communication, and boundaries that work for everyone.

The upgraded version 2.0 might take some getting used to, but the bugs in the old system weren't doing anyone any favors.

Love Is Love: Accepting Your Adult Child's Lifestyle Choices

Imagine your daughter announces she's quitting her law career to become a yoga instructor in Bali. Or your son introduces his new partner—all tattoos and blue hair—at Sunday dinner. Perhaps your adult child tells you they're gay, shattering not their identity, but the assumptions you held about it.

That sharp intake of breath you're holding? Time to let it out slowly.

It's all about perspective, how you frame it. Remember when they insisted on wearing their Superman cape to school? This isn't so different. Except now, instead of protecting them from playground snickers, you're learning to protect your relationship from your own preconceptions.

"But this isn't what we planned!" True. Neither was that time they painted their bedroom wall with crayon artwork, yet somehow you all survived. Today's challenge? Trading those carefully crafted dreams you had for them with support for the dreams they've chosen for themselves.

Here are a couple of Do's and Don'ts from the front lines:

DO:

- Ask questions with genuine curiosity
    - **Why:** Curiosity shows a willingness to understand without judgment.
- Acknowledge their courage in living authentically.
    - **Why:** When you validate their courage, you're affirming their right to pursue what feels meaningful to them.
- Express love, even when expressing concern

- - **Why:** Love and concern don't have to be mutually exclusive. By pairing your care with unconditional support, you show that your connection isn't tied to their choices.

- Share your wisdom when asked, not as ammunition
  - **Why:** It keeps your insights valued and prevents advice from feeling like control.

- Keep the door open for conversation
  - **Why:** An open door signals that you're a safe space, ready to listen whenever they need you.

DON'T:

- Start sentences with "In my day..."
  - **Why:** This can make your perspective seem outdated or irrelevant and make them feel judged.

- Compare them to their siblings or cousins
  - **Why:** Comparisons can feel dismissive of their individuality and create resentment.

- Use guilt as a persuasion tool
  - **Why:** Guilt undermines their confidence and can erode trust.

- Make acceptance conditional
  - **Why:** Conditional love can feel manipulative and erodes their sense of security in your relationship.

- Try to "fix" what isn't broken
  - **Why:** Attempting to change or "correct" their choices suggests a lack of faith in their judgment.

Let's say your son announces he's converting to a different religion. Instead of having heart failure and launching into why your family's faith tradition was good enough for generations, try: "I'd love to understand what about this faith speaks to you." See the difference? One response builds walls; the other builds bridges.

The secret is loving them for who they are, not who you imagined they'd be. Think of it like tending a garden—you can provide the best soil and conditions, but you can't control what kind of flower blooms. And isn't that the beauty of it? Your role isn't to approve or disapprove—it's to love. Sometimes that means biting your tongue so hard you can taste pennies. Other times it means defending their choices to Uncle Bob at Thanksgiving.

Always, it means choosing the relationship over being right.

Chapter 3:

The Art of Co-existing—

Sharing Spaces, Stronger Bonds

"Mom, is dinner at 6 or 7? And can Jake come over?"

Ah, the text messages that remind you your adult child still thinks you're running a bed-and-breakfast. Well, minus the breakfast, because they're sleeping until noon.

Living with adult children transforms the simplest interactions into a comedy of errors. That casual "family dinner" you planned? It's now a scheduling feat that requires more coordination than a NASA launch. Between your daughter's late work meetings, your son's gym sessions, and your own book club nights, finding time to break bread together feels like an enigma.

But these everyday moments—the chaotic dinner planning, the impromptu plus-ones, the Netflix battles over the living room TV—they're actually golden opportunities for connection. Not the forced, "let's-all-share-our-feelings" kind, but the real, messy, beautiful kind that happens when you least expect it. Think of it as family bonding for the modern age. Sure, it's not the picture-perfect scenes from those 90s sitcoms, but between the text chains and the takeout orders, there's magic in the mayhem.

Ready to turn those ordinary moments into something extraordinary? We're about to explore how to make togetherness happen without anyone feeling like they're trapped in a Hallmark movie.

Finding Balance: Negotiating Privacy and Autonomy

So your empty nest isn't so empty anymore. That "temporary" move back home has stretched longer than you expected, and suddenly you're wondering if those parental control settings from 2005 still apply.

Well, spoiler alert: they don't.

Your daughter's conducting Zoom meetings from the kitchen table while you're trying to make your morning smoothie. Your son's dating life now comes with a soundtrack of creaking floorboards at 2 a.m. Welcome to the delicate dance of sharing space with your adult offspring! Think of it like upgrading your operating system—Parent 1.0 worked great when they needed permission slips signed, but Parent 2.0 requires some serious updates to the privacy protocols.

Start with the physical stuff:

- create "no-barging-in" zones (their bedroom = their embassy)
- establish quiet hours
- design shared spaces with personal corners (that reading nook isn't going to create itself)
- set up privacy signals (headphones on = do not disturb)

But here's where it gets tricky—the emotional boundaries. Remember when you knew everything about their life because, well, you drove them everywhere? Now their social calendar is as mysterious as the internet algorithm.

Try these upgraded parenting moves:

- replace "Where are you going?" with "Hope you have fun!"
    - this allows you to offer support without acting like a detective
- swap "Let me help you with that" for "Need any input?"
    - this gives them the space to figure things out, while still being available if needed
- trade "In my experience..." for "How are you thinking about handling this?"
    - this opens the floor for them to share their thoughts rather than assuming they need advice
- exchange daily reports for weekly catch-ups
    - this is a more respectful way of maintaining connection without smothering their independence

Consider setting up house rules that respect everyone's autonomy. For instance:

- knock first, enter second
- text before bringing guests over—no surprise parties
- respect private conversations—the walls aren't getting any thicker
- honor personal schedules

They might still want your advice, but now it's more "optional update" than "required installation." Your job? Being available without being invasive, supportive without smothering, and present without hovering. Sure, you might still wake up in cold sweats wondering if they made it home safely. But instead of waiting up, maybe send a casual text:

"Door's unlocked if needed. Sleep well!" Because sometimes the best parenting happens when we parent less.

Think of privacy like Wi-Fi—everyone needs it, everyone uses it differently, and nobody likes it when it's interrupted. The password to this new living arrangement? R-E-S-P-E-C-T.

Mastering Conflict Resolution Under One Roof

Remember when their biggest meltdown was over a missing stuffed animal? Now you're both adults, sharing space, and somehow that discussion about whose turn it is to unload the dishwasher feels more explosive than a science fair volcano.

Well, here's your advanced course in family diplomacy, where every conversation has the potential to turn into either a productive discussion or an episode of a reality show we'd rather not star in. Think your United Nations peacekeeping skills peaked during their teenage years? Think again. Living with adult children brings on a whole new sequel to *Who Moved My Cheese*?

Let's break down the art of keeping peace without losing pieces:

1. **Communication Game-Changers**

    a. Trade "You always..." for "I feel..."

        i. Shifting from blame to emotion makes it easier for your adult child to hear you without immediately going into defensive mode.

    b. Swap "Back in my day..." for "What's your take on this?"

        i. Inviting opinions instead of pushing them encourages collaboration and mutual respect.

      c. Replace door slams with time-outs

           i. It's all about cooling off before saying something regrettable.

      d. Exchange silent treatments for scheduled talks

           i. Allows everyone to voice concerns, ensuring nothing festers in silence.

2. **House Rules That Actually Work**

      a. No conflict discussions after 9 p.m.—tired minds = loose cannons

      b. Designated "cool-down" spaces for each person

      c. 24-hour rule on bringing up issues

      d. Monthly family meetings

Let's scan over a couple of real-life scenarios:

- When they leave dishes in the sink: "I notice the kitchen gets cluttered by evening. Could we brainstorm a system that works for everyone?"

- Instead of "Your music is too loud!" try "I'm having trouble focusing. Can we figure out quiet hours that work for both of us?"

- Rather than "You never chip in!" consider "Let's create a shared expenses spreadsheet."

The secret is active listening. Not the "nodding while mentally composing your rebuttal" kind, but genuine "I hear you" moments. When your daughter explains why she needs the car every Tuesday, resist the urge to remind her about your schedule first. When your son defends his midnight snacking habits, take a breath before launching into your lecture about kitchen cleanliness.

Conflict resolution is like a dance—sometimes you lead, sometimes you follow, but it always works better when both partners are in sync. And yes, occasionally someone steps on toes, but that's how you learn the steps. You're not failing if conflicts arise—you're only failing if you avoid addressing them.

The goal isn't to eliminate disagreements (good luck with that!) but to handle them with the grace of someone who's been practicing this parenting thing for a few decades.

Discussing the Strain on Relationships

Remember those early parenting years when you'd steal kisses during naptime? When the house was finally quiet, and you could breathe for a moment? Well, your adult child might not nap anymore—though wouldn't that be nice? —but you still need those moments of connection. Except now, instead of hiding from a toddler, you're juggling schedules, timing your coffee dates around your daughter's work-from-home calls or your son's post-gym protein shake ritual. It's not just a scheduling challenge; it's a relationship evolution.

The marital mattress? Feels like it's turned into a tightrope, doesn't it? One partner whispers, "They need to move out," while the other murmurs, "They just need more time." Meanwhile, your romantic life requires more strategic planning than a military operation. Spontaneity? It's been replaced by whispered planning sessions in the kitchen, covert text messages, and date nights that feel like smuggling moments of joy past the ever-present shadow of adulthood in your living room.

But here's the silver lining: You're not alone in this balancing act. Let's talk marriage survival strategies. These little tweaks aren't just helpful—they're lifelines:

1. **Couple-Time Tactics**

    a. Morning coffee dates before the house wakes up

    b. Evening walks—adult kids rarely volunteer for those, trust me

    c. Code words for "We need alone time"

    d. Regular date nights—no tag-a-longs allowed

    e. Weekend escapes—even if it's to a local Airbnb

2. **Dividing and Conquering**

    a. Create a shared calendar for household management

    b. Split parent-child communications fairly

    c. Take turns being the "bad guy" when needed

    d. Share financial decisions about supporting your child

    e. Alternate who handles challenging conversations

3. **Supporting Each Other Through the Chaos**

    a. Regular check-ins about feelings and frustrations

    b. Always maintain a united front on house rules

    c. Private space for venting—away from vulnerable ears

    d. Appreciation moments for each other's patience

    e. Stress-relief activities you both enjoy

Your marriage is like a garden that needs regular tending, even when there's an extra tree casting shade. Water it daily with small gestures—a knowing wink across the dinner table, a subtle hand squeeze during family movie night, or leaving love notes in unexpected places.

Remember: You fell in love before they came along, and you'll stay in love after they (eventually) leave again. Your relationship needs nurturing now more than ever. Those stolen moments between work calls and laundry loads? They're not selfish—they're essential. And here's a radical thought: Maybe this unexpected family reunion is actually an opportunity to show your adult child what a healthy, resilient partnership looks like.

You're still modeling life skills—including how to keep love alive.

Blended Families and Step-Children

Imagine trying to merge two different playlists into one harmonious soundtrack. Mmm, rather tricky. Blended family life is pretty much the same thing. Instead of mixing pop with classical, you're blending family traditions, parenting styles, and occasionally clashing personalities.

Oh, and everyone's an adult now, with their own firmly established ideas about how things should work.

Your stepdaughter's moving back in with her own playlist of expectations, while your son's still adjusting to sharing the family photo wall with new faces. Meanwhile, you're wondering if it's possible to love "Baby Shark" and death metal equally. Totally possible, but it takes practice and patience. Building relationships with adult stepchildren feels like joining a book club halfway through the novel—you've missed some crucial chapters, but you're eager to be part of the story. The trick? Don't try to rewrite their earlier chapters; focus on co-authoring the ones ahead.

1. **Relationship Building That Actually Works**

    a. Skip the "instant family" pressure because forcing closeness can backfire; relationships need time to grow naturally—rushed efforts can leave you with a sticky mess.

    b. Create new traditions without erasing old ones to honor everyone's past. This creates a sense of continuity while forging shared experiences to help build a new family narrative.

c. Find common ground (even if it's complaining about dad jokes). This is the ultimate icebreaker and a shortcut to connection.

d. Respect pre-existing parent-child bonds, focusing on your unique role to foster harmony instead.

e. Build one-on-one connections naturally, eliminating the added pressure of performing for an audience concerning group dynamics.

2. **Merging Family Values**

    a. Family meetings where everyone gets a voice and ensure that no one feels sidelined in their own home.

    b. Shared meals with rotating menu planners, turning a mundane task into a bonding activity, plus it showcases everyone's tastes and traditions.

    c. Holiday celebrations that honor multiple traditions to keep everyone's culture alive while creating new memories to share as a family.

    d. House rules that respect everyone's comfort zones reduce misunderstandings and help everyone feel safe in their shared space.

    e. Flexible routines that bend before they break, respecting everyone's unique schedules and needs and preventing resentment from rigid systems.

3. **Tension-Taming Techniques**

    a. Neutral zones in shared spaces where everyone feels comfortable will reduce territorial disputes.

b. Clear communication channels to prevent misunderstandings and build trust.

c. Private time for original family units, allowing existing bonds to thrive without anyone feeling overshadowed by the new dynamics.

d. Equal treatment in practical matters to eliminate feelings of favoritism which can derail even the strongest relationships.

e. Respect for different attachment speeds, and allowing time helps ensure genuine bonds, not just surface-level peace.

That scene in *The Brady Bunch* where everything works out perfectly in 30 minutes? Yeah, real life works differently. Your stepson might not want to call you "Mom," and that's okay. Your daughter might need time to accept sharing holiday traditions. Growth happens in small moments—like when your stepdaughter asks for your recipe, or your son includes his step-siblings in game night.

Blending families is pretty much like making soup—some ingredients take longer to soften than others, but rushing the process only leads to undercooked results. Some days you're the chef, carefully stirring the pot; other days you're the taste tester, sampling new flavors with an open mind. Success isn't measured by how quickly everyone bonds, but by how authentically relationships develop. The key lies in understanding that "family" can expand without anyone losing their place in the original recipe.

After all, isn't the best part of blending families the chance to prove that love multiplies rather than divides?

Living With Grandchildren: Bridging the Generation Gap

Well, well, well, would you look at that! Your house has turned into a time-traveling adventure, and you're the captain of this multigenerational ship.

Grandpa's regaling the kids with tales about rotary phones and Saturday morning cartoons while the five-year-old explains the finer points of unlocking an iPad. Meanwhile, your teenager rolls their eyes at both, earbuds firmly in place. Your living room has become the epicenter of a cultural exchange program—except everyone's related, and nobody gets to leave.

This is the reality of a three-generation household. Dinner conversations bounce between TikTok trends and "back in my day" anecdotes, and navigating it all can feel like hosting a daily summit of the United Nations of Family Life. It's chaotic, yes—but it's also filled with opportunities for connection, learning, and plenty of laughter.

Think your parenting skills peaked with your own kids? Think again.

Now, you're juggling the unique challenge of explaining to Grandma why the grandkids need screen time for their school projects, while convincing your little one that Grandpa's prized vinyl record player isn't a DJ station. It's like running a crash course in diplomacy, with you as the mediator between the past and the present. The magic, though, lies in the moments where these generations collide—and, unexpectedly, connect. It's in Grandpa's surprised grin when he masters a video game controller, or when your teenager asks Grandma for her cookie recipe and actually follows it. It's in the quiet "Aha!" moments when stories of the past meet the tech of today, creating memories that will span generations.

But it's not all sunshine and homemade cookies. Differences in values, parenting styles, and expectations can spark friction faster than you can say "family meeting." So how do you turn the challenges into chances for deeper bonds?

By shifting the narrative. Trade judgment for curiosity, criticism for connection, and eye rolls for genuine interest. When you swap "That's not how we did it" for "Show me how that works," you're opening a door to unexpected learning moments, where clashes become conversations and misunderstandings turn into opportunities for growth. It's not just about managing a generation gap—it's about building a generation bridge. Whether you're orchestrating a family history scavenger hunt, tackling tech-teaching sessions, or blending Grandma's know-how with modern-day flair in the garden, every interaction becomes a chance to strengthen those ties.

At the end of the day, this multigenerational mix isn't just a logistical challenge—it's a gift. It's about creating a space where wisdom flows both ways, stories intertwine, and every member of the family feels like they belong. Because in this recipe of life, every ingredient matters, and when blended just right, the result is pure magic.

1. **Making Peace Across the Ages**

    a. Trade judgment for curiosity about different perspectives. This opens the door to unexpected learning moments, turning clashes into conversations.

    b. Swap "That's not how we did it" for "Show me how that works." This lets each generation feel seen and valued for their unique experiences.

    c. Replace eye rolls with genuine interest to invite mutual understanding.

    d. Exchange criticism for conversation, turning misunderstandings into opportunities for growth.

2. **Activities That Actually Work**

    a. Family history scavenger hunts, especially those embarrassing photos. This creates laughter and bonds while showcasing each generation's quirks.

    b. Tech-teaching sessions to empower younger and older generations alike. (Grandpa might surprise you with his gaming skills).

    c. Recipe-sharing adventures merge nostalgia with creativity, producing memories as sweet as the cookies themselves (and, nobody makes cookies like Grandma).

    d. Garden-to-table projects because traditional know-how with modern flair builds teamwork and yields delicious results.

    e. Story-swapping sessions to blend past and present. This creates a living family history everyone can enjoy.

3. **Role-Defining Without the Drama**

    a. Clear caregiving boundaries to ensure everyone knows when to step in—or step back.

    b. Designated teaching territories to make each person's contribution feel purposeful and appreciated.

    c. Balanced authority (because "Ask Grandma" shouldn't trump house rules). This consistency strengthens respect for everyone's role while preventing power struggles.

    d. Scheduled alone time for each generation to allow individuals to recharge, ensuring harmony in shared spaces.

    e. Shared decision-making on family matters to help foster unity and show that everyone's voice matters.

When was the last time three generations had so much to teach each other? Treating each generation like they've got something valuable to bring to the table—because they do. It's like a perfect recipe where every ingredient matters.

You're not managing a generation gap—you're building a generation bridge. Sometimes that means being the translator between "What's the tea?" and "How about some coffee?" Other times, it means stepping back and watching the magic happen.

At the end of the day, it's about creating a space where wisdom flows both ways, stories intertwine, and everyone feels like they belong.

Extending an Invitation to Connect:
Making Opportunities for Togetherness

Forget the awkward silences and smartphone-dominated interactions. Family connection isn't about grand gestures—it's about transforming mundane moments into memories. And where there's a will, there's always a way. Let's look at a couple of creative strategies to make memories:

- **Build an Outdoor Bar: More Than Wood and Nails**

Power tools are scattered, Dad is cracking dad jokes, and your young adult child is rolling their eyes but secretly loving every moment. Building an outdoor bar becomes less about the finished product and more about the collaborative chaos. Each hammer swing, each misaligned board, creates an undercurrent of teamwork that'll be retold at future family gatherings.

- **Re-decorating the Adult Child's Bedroom: A Canvas of Compromise**

This isn't just about paint swatches and throw pillows. This is where personal expression and mutual respect meet. Your adult child gets to stamp their evolving identity onto the space, while you provide guidance and the occasional funding, of course. Welcome to the ultimate design collaboration.

- **Learning New Hobbies Together: Embracing Collective Awkwardness**

Who says you can't teach an old dog new tricks—or a twenty-something how to appreciate family time? Cooking classes where a deflating soufflé becomes a shared laugh. Kayaking expeditions where getting soaked is part of the bonding process. Tennis games where the witty banter keeps the match in play. These aren't just activities, they're vulnerability workshops disguised as fun.

- **Spending Time in Nature: Unplugged and Unfiltered**

Hiking trails become a sanctuary of genuine conversation as the landscape becomes a neutral mediator. Suddenly, discussing life's complexities feels less confrontational and more collaborative.

- **Monthly Shopping Trips: Retail Therapy Meets Family Therapy**

Forget the stereotype of teenage eye-rolling. These trips are strategic connection points. Farmer's markets, mall wanderings, vintage store explorations—each outing is a micro-adventure in understanding each other's tastes and priorities.

It's not about perfection. It's about the spontaneous conversations that bloom during shared focus. That moment when fixing a broken shelf transforms into a deep discussion about life goals. These interactions can't be scripted—they're organic, unexpected, beautiful. Traditions aren't about rigidity; they're about rhythm. Sunday dinner where everyone contributes a dish. Annual camping trips. Seasonal family photoshoots where matching outfits are mandatory (and slightly cringeworthy). These rituals become the glue that holds families together and create memories that can always be fondly looked back upon.

The only thing? Stop trying so hard. Connection happens in the unscripted moments, the shared laughter, the collective eye-rolls. Your family isn't a project to be managed—it's a living, breathing ecosystem of love, frustration, and unwavering support.

Chapter 4:

Effective Communication—

How to Connect and Have

Real Conversations

Your son left wet towels on the bathroom floor—again. Your first instinct? Channel your inner drill sergeant and launch into that well-rehearsed speech about responsibility. But before you unleash years of pent-up laundry frustration, let's pause that reaction reel.

Remember last week's towel standoff? The one that somehow spiraled into a greatest-hits compilation of every chore left undone since 2015, culminating in slammed doors and silent dinners? Yeah, that's not exactly the "adult relationship" you imagined when they moved back home. Here's the thing about living with adult children: those little irritations aren't really about wet towels or unwashed dishes. They're smoke signals warning of bigger fires—unmet expectations, boundary battles, and the delicate dance of treating your child like the adult they've become.

Think of communication as your family's operating system. When it crashes, everything freezes; respect, understanding, growth—even your ability to enjoy each other's company. Nobody wants their home to feel like a passive-aggressive war zone where every interaction carries the weight of unspoken tensions.

So, let's look into how you can turn those communication landmines into building blocks.

The Power of Active Listening: When "I Hear You" Actually Means You're Listening

Perhaps you find yourself in a situation where your daughter's explaining why she quit her stable office job to pursue freelance photography. Your brain's already composing a PowerPoint presentation titled "Why This Is Financial Suicide," complete with pie charts and retirement projections.

But hold that thought—actually, hold all the thoughts.

Active listening isn't about perfecting your poker face while mentally drafting your rebuttal. It's about putting your parental pause button exactly where it belongs—on your instinct to fix, direct, or protect. Think of it as upgrading from Parent 1.0—where you had all the answers—to Parent 2.0—where sometimes the best answer is no answer at all.

Why does this matter?

Because your adult child can smell inauthentic listening from a mile away. That subtle phone check during their relationship crisis? They saw it. That half-hearted "mm-hmm" while you sorted mail? They felt it. Each distracted moment sends a clear message: "Your words matter less than this electric bill."

Here's your field guide to genuine listening:

Stop playing conversation tennis. You know the game—they serve up a problem, and you volley back advice before their words finish echoing. Instead, try this revolutionary approach: actual silence. Let their words land. Marinate in them. React to them after they've finished their complete thought.

Nonverbal cues scream "I'm here" louder than any words could:

- Maintain eye contact.

- - Don't multitask or check your phone.
- Let them finish speaking.
  - Don't jump to conclusions or interrupt.
- Paraphrase or summarize what your child says to confirm understanding.
  - Don't downplay or dismiss their feelings.
- Use nonverbal cues like nodding to show engagement.
  - Refrain from any sarcasm, negativity, judgment, or disinterest whether verbally or non-verbally.
- Ask clarifying questions if needed.
  - Don't offer any unsolicited advice immediately.

When you do speak, make it count. "So what I'm hearing is..." followed by their words—not your interpretation—shows you're tracking their story, not writing your own version.

For example:

Child: "I'm thinking about moving to Seattle."

Parent Brain (Silenced): But it rains there! Your seasonal depression! The cost of living!

Parent Voice (Activated): "Tell me more about what draws you to Seattle."

Understand that active listening isn't about abandoning your wisdom—it's about creating space for their wisdom to emerge. Sometimes the best parenting happens when we park our solutions at the door and trust that our adult children might actually know what they're talking about.

Speaking Without Criticism

Remember when your parents' criticism made you instantly see the error of your ways and immediately transform into a model citizen? No? Funny how that works.

Yet here you are, channeling your inner critic, certain that pointing out every misstep will somehow spark an "aha!" moment in your adult child. Simply put: it won't. Those well-crafted lectures about responsibility? They're hitting your adult child's ears like a mainstream hit song they've heard way too many times.

Criticism lands like a lead balloon because your adult child isn't sitting there thinking, "Wow, Mom/Dad really nailed it with that devastating analysis of my financial choices!" They're mentally packing their bags for a guilt trip while building walls higher than their student loan debt.

What to do?

- Focus on the behavior, not the person.
- Replace harsh statements with neutral observations.
- Offer solutions instead of blame.

Picture these two scenes:

- **Scene 1 (The Crash and Burn):**
    - **Parent:** "You're never going to save money if you keep buying $7 lattes!"
    - **Child:** Immediately downloads food delivery app out of spite.
- **Scene 2 (The Actually Helpful Version):**
    - **Parent:** "I found some great coffee recipes on TikTok. Want to try making our own fancy drinks?"

- **Child:** Might actually consider it because nobody's attacking their life choices.

Curiosity over judgment. Questions over declarations. Support over shame.

Think of criticism as a boomerang—it always comes back to smack you in the face. Your adult child doesn't need a personal critic; they need a parent who can point out the stars while they're counting the dark places.

Using "I" Statements: Because "You" Statements Won't Cut It

Remember when you could solve any problem with "Because I said so"? Simpler times, right? Now your adult child has opinions and rebuttals—and sometimes they're actually right!

This is the era where communication needs more finesse than a diplomatic summit.

Turns out, starting sentences with "you" is like pulling the pin on a conversational grenade. "You never clean up!" BAM! Defensive walls up. "You're always late!" BOOM! Eye rolls deployed. "You don't respect my house!" EXPLOSION! Welcome to Silent Treatment City, population: the entire household. But here's where "I" statements swoop in like the communication heroes they are. Instead of pointing fingers, you're sharing your experience. It's the difference between declaring war and opening negotiations.

The "I" Statement Formula

1. State your feelings
2. Identify the situation/behavior causing the feelings

3. Discuss the impact the situation/behavior has on you

4. Express what you need/prefer

Here are a couple of "from blame game to brain gain" examples:

Blame Game	Brain Gain
"You're destroying my kitchen!"	"I feel anxious when the kitchen's messy because I can't find what I need to cook dinner. Could we work out a cleanup system?"
"You're taking advantage of free rent!"	"I feel concerned when expenses aren't shared because it impacts our household budget. Can we discuss financial contributions?"
"You're avoiding family time!"	"I feel sad when we miss family dinners because those moments matter to me. What schedule might work better for you?"
"You don't respect my rules!"	"I feel frustrated when house guidelines aren't followed because it affects everyone's comfort. How can we create rules that work for all of us?"

"I" statements aren't magic spells that instantly transform your adult child into a responsible human. They're more like bridges—they might not guarantee someone will cross, but at least you're not burning them down with accusations.

And sometimes, that's enough to start a real conversation.

Creating Safe Spaces for Honest Conversations

Your young adult is hovering in the doorway, doing that familiar dance of "I need to tell you something but I'd rather eat glass." The last time you saw this expression, he/she was confessing to that fender bender in high school. Now at 25, somehow, the stakes feel even higher.

Creating a safe space isn't about throwing down emotional pillows and brewing chamomile tea. It's about transforming your home from a potential judgment zone into a place where hard truths can land softly—both parties feel comfortable sharing thoughts and feelings without fear of criticism, judgment, or anger.

The setup matters so be sure to check the following boxes in order to create a safe space for communication:

- Choose a neutral time and place for discussions.
- Avoid distractions.
- Commit to staying calm, even if emotions run high.
- Acknowledge their feelings without immediately trying to "fix" the problem.

And, along with this, there are a couple of golden rules to follow:

- Treat their words like fine china—handle with care.
- Let silence be your copilot.
- Keep your face in "supportive listener" mode, not "preparing counterarguments" mode.
- Just remember: Understanding doesn't always mean agreeing.

Your role isn't to be their personal problem solver. You're more like an emotional safe house—a place where they can unpack their baggage without you immediately trying to reorganize it.

When your adult child feels safe sharing their struggles, you're not losing control—you're gaining their trust. Even if sometimes that means biting your tongue so hard you need dental work.

Clear agreements replace guilt with respect. Boundaries show love, not control.

Chapter 5:

Practical Tips—Paying their Way

"Mom, I can't afford rent this month... again."

These are five words that can turn your carefully balanced budget into an emotional hostage situation. One minute you're planning that long-overdue kitchen renovation, the next you're wondering if your retirement fund can handle another "temporary" loan. Meanwhile, your partner's giving you that look—the one that screams "We talked about this!"

Money conversations with adult children feel about as comfortable as a root canal without anesthesia. You're torn between wanting to help and wondering if your support is more enabler than empowerment. Your head says "tough love," but your heart whispers "What's another month?"

The stakes?

Higher than the sky. We're talking about more than dollars and cents here—we're dealing in trust, independence, and those Sunday family dinners that suddenly feel charged with unspoken tension. One mishandled conversation about shared groceries can spiral into years of passive-aggressive comments about who ate the last yogurt.

That's why this chapter is your financial survival guide for the modern family shuffle. Time to figure out where your wallet ends and their financial future begins.

Let's look into those numbers—and all the feelings hiding behind them.

Paying Rent

"Wait, you want me to charge my own child rent? I might as well bill them for hugs, then."

This is the financial tango of parenting, where love meets fiscal responsibility—otherwise known as the financial dance of adulting. Charging rent has nothing to do with squeezing a couple of dollars from your offspring—it's about equipping them with real-world financial literacy.

Think of it as a "sense of responsibility" investment.

- **The 50% Rule: Math Meets Mercy**

Forget random numbers pulled from thin air. The 50% rule is a superb financial compass. Calculate market-rate rent in your area, then request half. Why? You're creating a safety net with training wheels. We need real-world scenarios here, people.

For example, if a studio apartment costs $1,500 locally, ask for $750. This approach accomplishes three critical things:

- **Provides a meaningful financial contribution:** Asking them to chip in makes them feel like an active participant in the household economy. This isn't Monopoly money—it's their hard-earned cash going toward a tangible expense. It's a good taste of reality.

- **Teaches budgeting skills:** With rent in the mix, they'll have to think twice before blowing their paycheck on all those "nice-to-haves." It's about practical financial discipline.

- **Keeps their savings intact:** Keeping rent at 50% allows them to save while still experiencing the reality of regular financial obligations.

- **Bonus for you:** And hey, I bet it's even going to teach some negotiation skills.

Pro tip: Base the amount on their actual income. A part-time barista paying $750 looks different from a junior programmer's contribution.

- **Adult Tenant Mindset: More Than Blood Ties**

Flip the script. They're not just your child—they're a roommate with genetic privileges. Professionalism prevents emotional landmines.

This mindset shifts the dynamics where you negotiate shared spaces. It's a small mental tweak with big benefits for their self-esteem and independence. Imagine running a small, very loving bed-and-breakfast where occasionally someone leaves dirty socks on the floor. Your job? Maintain boundaries while offering unconditional support. Treating your child like an adult tenant helps them adapt to the realities of living with others.

And, when emotions are removed from the rent equation, what's left is mutual respect.

- **Trial Period: The Independent Test**

Before they boomerang home, propose a six-month solo mission. Can they manage utilities? Pay bills on time? This reconnaissance reveals their true financial capability.

Think of it like a financial boot camp. Some kids crush it; others might realize budgeting is harder than it looks. Either way, it's better they learn under your guidance than face eviction notices down the line.

If they flounder, it's a chance to recalibrate. Maybe they need more time at home or a budget refresher course. What's important is that you'll both know where they stand.

- **The Contract Approach: Bureaucracy Meets Family**

Yes, a written agreement sounds coldly corporate. But nothing says "I take you seriously" like a documented understanding. A signed agreement signals that you're serious about this arrangement. It's not a casual suggestion; it's a commitment.

Someday, they'll be signing an actual lease with a landlord who doesn't forgive late payments or tolerate unwashed dishes. This is their practice round.

Critical contract components include:

- **Exact rent amount and due date:** Because tracking payment deadlines is part of "adulting."
- **Utility cost-sharing:** Whether it's splitting the electric bill or contributing to the Netflix account, they'll learn the cost of convenience.
- **Cleaning expectations:** Say hello to shared accountability.
- **Late payment consequences:** A small penalty teaches them real-world lessons about financial discipline.

Pro move: Treat this like a real lease. Professionalism doesn't negate love—it amplifies respect.

- **Clarity and Deadline: No Ambiguity Allowed**

When introducing rent, channel your inner HR manager. Be clear, direct, and compassionate.

Here's a quick script framework:

- "Here's what I'm thinking about your living situation. [Explain rent logic]
- The amount is [X], due on [date].
- I'm doing this because I love you and want you financially strong."

Remember, you're not extracting money. You're investing in their future, one rent check at a time.

This isn't about dollars. It's about transformation. You're teaching financial adulting through lived experience. Your adult child might grumble. They might roll their eyes. But years later, they'll appreciate the real-world training ground you provided—right in your living room.

Rent isn't a punishment. It's preparation.

Shared Expenses and Utilities

Returning home doesn't mean returning to free room service. Shared living requires shared financial responsibility—a concept more complicated than quantum physics for most twenty-somethings.

Shared Resources: The Invisible Price Tag

Every Wi-Fi connection, every refrigerator raid, and every load of laundry carries a cost. If you can stay you can pay; your adult child needs a crash course in household economics.

Here's a quick calculation strategy for you to sample:

- Estimate monthly utility costs
- Divide proportionally based on usage
- Create a transparent spreadsheet
- Review together monthly

Pro tip: Use actual bills as visual aids. Nothing says "real world" like itemized electricity statements.

Gradual Financial Responsibility: The Incremental Approach

You don't want to shock them into oblivion. Be reasonable and think of financial integration like training wheels. Start gently and build momentum. For instance:

- **Month One: Grocery Contributions**
    - Assign specific shopping trips
    - Request percentage of food budget
    - Encourage meal planning
- **Month Two: Personal Expenses**
    - Mobile phone bill
    - Streaming subscriptions
    - Personal care products
- **Month Three: Utility Contributions**
    - Partial electricity payment
    - Internet cost-sharing
    - Gas or heating expenses

Real Consequences: Economic Reality Check

Financial freeloading has systemic impacts and your household isn't an infinite fountain of financial resources.

Some potential family financial constraints you can expect include:

- reduced vacation budgets

- delayed home repairs
- limited dining experiences
- restricted personal savings

Communicate candidly: Their non-participation affects everyone's lifestyle. Economic ecosystems require collective responsibility. As mentioned, this isn't punishment, it's preparation. You're transforming dependency into mutual respect, transforming a bedroom into an economic classroom.

Your goal?

Equip them with financial literacy while maintaining familial warmth. Some lessons require spreadsheets, others require compassion.

Shared expenses aren't about extracting money. They're about building economic citizenship—one utility bill at a time. This brings us to our next topic: addressing financial irresponsibility.

Addressing Financial Irresponsibility

Ah, the tough love ledger. Look, financial literacy isn't inherited—it's engineered. It's learned and it's earned. Transforming a spending hurricane into a budgetary breeze requires strategic intervention.

If your adult child's wallet resembles a crime scene, it's time for some economic CPR. I'm talking about the "essentials versus non-essentials" exercise. Time to do the math:

- **Must-Have Expenses**
    - Electricity
    - Groceries
    - Basic healthcare

- Transportation

- **Luxury Elimination Zone**
    - Streaming subscriptions
    - Takeout marathons
    - Designer coffee expeditions
    - Impulse online shopping

Brutal but brilliant strategy: Remove non-essential conveniences until financial responsibility emerges.

Another strategy that works wonders is making use of an incentivized timeline approach. Think of it as a responsibility boot camp:

- **Month One: Internet Contribution**
    - Research actual cost
    - Demonstrate billing
    - Connect payment to usage

- **Month Two: Grocery Investment**
    - Assign specific shopping responsibilities
    - Introduce meal planning
    - Track spending patterns

- **Month Three: Transportation Costs**
    - Shared fuel expenses
    - Public transit contributions
    - Maintenance cost awareness

This isn't punishment. It's financial rehabilitation. You're transforming a cash-burning butterfly into a budgeting eagle. Some lessons require spreadsheets. Others require patience. Most require both.

Retired Parents and Finances

Your retirement isn't a financial free-for-all for your adult children. Retirement represents your hard-earned economic sovereignty. Your bank account isn't a family charity—those hard-earned dollars are your lifetime achievement trophy.

From Parental ATM to Economic Boundary Setter

Decades of financial support don't obligate perpetual subsidization. You've funded childhoods, education, and early adulthoods. Your retirement isn't a continuation of that funding model.

These conversations will inevitably arise where your funds are questioned, so it's important to have a few solid strategies ready—like key communication points you can confidently deploy when the moment of truth arrives. Your retirement is about reclaiming your time, your energy, and yes, your finances.

- **Acknowledge past support:** The big words here are "past support" not "lifetime contract." You've done the heavy lifting—now it's their turn to stand on their own two feet. Recognize and celebrate how far they've come with your help.

- **Emphasize current financial constraints:** Explain that retirement brings a shift in financial priorities.

- **Highlight retirement as a personal milestone:** This is your time to focus on yourself—it's not about cutting them off; it's about a well-deserved pivot.

- **Reinforce economic independence expectations:** Make it clear that financial independence is a crucial part of their own growth. Setting economic boundaries isn't selfish—it's an act of love that teaches them self-reliance and accountability.

Contribution Strategies: Respect Meets Reality

Remember, as mentioned, financial boundaries aren't emotional barriers. They're economic guardrails protecting both generations. Without boundaries, your nest egg becomes their safety net, leaving you vulnerable.

Some good implementation tactics worth a try include:

- Transparent expense discussions
- Consistent contribution expectations
- Gradual responsibility transfer
- Clear communication of limitations

This isn't abandonment. It's economic emancipation. You're teaching self-sufficiency through strategic disengagement. Your retirement isn't a finish line. It's a brand-new starting point—where your financial health takes center stage.

Your wallet. Your rules.

Encourage Saving and Financial Planning

Well, with all that said, financial independence isn't a destination either—it's a carefully crafted skill set. Your role? Master architect of economic wisdom.

Savings Accountability: The Balanced Contribution Model

Debt repayment (student loans and credit cards for instance) doesn't exempt economic participation. Even small contributions build massive psychological muscles, impacting their mindset and habits. It's not about the amount; it's about fostering a mindset of responsibility.

Strategic Approach

- **Fixed percentage contributions:** Instead of an arbitrary amount, ask for a percentage of their income—say, 10–20%. This keeps things fair and adaptable to their financial situation.

- **Consistent expectation enforcement:** It builds trust and eliminates confusion.

- **Recognition of debt management efforts:** Encouragement reinforces good habits.

- **Proportional expectations based on income:** If they're earning minimum wage, contributions will naturally be lower. Tailor expectations to their earnings to avoid undue financial strain.

Your Comfort Zone: The Surprise Savings Hack

Feeling guilty about charging your young adult child rent? Simply transform potential guilt into strategic generosity. Consider a covert savings plan:

1. Collect "rent" payments

2. Secretly deposit into a separate account

3. Create a future financial cushion

4. Voila, potential graduation or emergency fund surprise

This approach accomplishes two big goals at once: It holds them accountable for contributing to household expenses while also ensuring they have a safety net when they need it most.

Long-Term Vision: Planting Economic Seeds

Raising financially independent adults is about equipping them with the knowledge and skills to think big—like, "retire at 50 and travel the world" big. Life's about more than just paying the bills on time.

Critical Financial Conversations:

- **Emergency fund strategies:** Explain the importance of having 3–6 months' worth of living expenses saved. Even $10 a week adds up over time.

- **Debt elimination techniques:** Teach them to tackle high-interest debt first, understand the snowball or avalanche methods, and avoid credit card pitfalls.

- **Retirement planning basics:** Even if they're in their 20s, a quick lesson on 401(k)s, Roth IRAs, and compound interest can set them on a lucrative path.

- **Investment fundamentals:** Introduce them to low-risk investments, index funds, and the magic of passive income.

- **Credit score management:** Show them how to monitor their credit, avoid unnecessary hard inquiries, and pay bills on time to keep their score healthy.

Budgeting isn't boring. It's financial self-defense. Your mission: Transform economic uncertainty into calculated confidence—one conversation at a time.

Dealing with Job Loss and Unemployment

Let's get one thing clear: Unemployment isn't a vacation—it's a full-time job-hunting mission. It's a time to rebuild, regroup, and reemerge stronger.

Temporary setbacks don't equal permanent residence in the parental support system. Instead, this is the proving ground where economic resilience begins.

Alternative Contributions: Sweat Equity Matters

When paychecks pause, contributions don't have to—household contributions become currency. Yes, right now, sweat equity is the coin of the times.

Think of it as creating a "Chore Portfolio" where value isn't measured in dollars but in deeds.

For instance:

- Lawn maintenance
- Home repairs
- Meal preparation
- Deep cleaning
- Vehicle maintenance
- Administrative tasks

It works because it keeps them engaged, and accountable, and provides a psychological boost by demonstrating productivity and value.

And that, dear parent, is how you transform unemployment into productive opportunity.

Focus on Progress: Motivation Through Celebration

Micro-achievements deserve macro-recognition. If we're honest for a hot second, job-hunting isn't exactly a walk in the park and motivation fuels momentum in this regard.

Here are a couple of wins well worth celebrating:

- **Resume refinement:** Polished CV? That's step one to career resurrection.

- **Skill certification completion:** Online courses and certifications = future job ammunition.

- **Networking connections:** That LinkedIn message could land the next big lead.

- **Interview preparation:** Practice might not make perfect, but it does make progress.

- **Professional development workshops:** Learning today to earn tomorrow.

Always remember, positive reinforcement trumps criticism every single time.

Support Their Search: Collaborative Empowerment

Your role: Strategic advisor, not rescue helicopter. Be the wind beneath their wings, not the crutch beneath their arms.

Some great guidance strategies include:

- **Resume workshop sessions:** Help them highlight their best self on paper.

- **Mock interview practice:** Familiarity breeds comfort.

- **Industry connection introductions:** A well-placed referral can work wonders.

- **Skill assessment discussions:** Help them identify areas for growth that align with job market demands.

- **Professional network insights:** Share wisdom from your own career path—what worked, what didn't.

Unemployment is temporary. Economic resilience is permanent.

Balancing Financial Support With Self-Sufficiency: The Collaborative Contribution Model

You're about to become a financial fairy godparent—minus the magic wand, plus spreadsheets!

Supporting without enabling is an art, and your masterpiece is fostering independence. Partial support isn't a weakness. It's strategic empowerment.

Here are a couple of support scenarios to get the ball rolling:

- **50% car payment contingent on employment:** Wheels are essential for job searches, but effort earns the ride.

- **Matching savings contributions:** Dollar-for-dollar motivation builds good habits fast.

- **Proportional assistance based on income:** Keep it fair and realistic for both sides.

- **Performance-linked financial support:** Tie financial help to measurable progress, like job applications or interview attendance.

- **Gradual reduction of assistance:** Ease them off the support ladder one rung at a time.

Celebrate Growth: The Confidence Catalyst

Why do we love milestones? Because every step forward is worth a fist bump—or maybe even a champagne toast!

Some milestone recognitions might include:

- Debt elimination celebrations
- Savings achievement acknowledgments
- Professional development kudos
- Financial independence markers

Positive reinforcement creates economic momentum. Remember, your mission is to transform financial dependence into autonomous confidence—strategically, compassionately, and mathematically.

Neurodivergent Support: The Compassionate Adaptation Guide

Welcome to the advanced class of neuro-inclusive economic strategy. Neurodiversity transforms financial independence into a complex landscape where traditional economic frameworks collide with unique cognitive processing styles. Parents of neurodivergent adult children must craft personalized strategies that balance financial expectations with a thorough understanding of individual neurological differences.

This approach demands extraordinary patience, precision, and a radical reimagining of economic skill-building.

- Communication becomes intricate—requiring language that is simultaneously clear, calm, and meticulously structured to prevent sensory overwhelm or emotional escalation. Visual aids, written expectations, and carefully crafted verbal explanations become critical translation tools, bridging potential misunderstandings between neurotypical expectations and neurodivergent experiences.

- Financial tasks must be deconstructed into microscopic, achievable milestones that transform potential anxiety into incremental confidence. Each small victory—whether understanding a bank statement, managing a modest budget, or completing a financial application—represents a significant breakthrough in economic autonomy.

- Tailored timelines replace rigid structures, acknowledging that skill development occurs through personalized learning paths uniquely calibrated to individual cognitive strengths and potential challenges.

- Sensory considerations become paramount: Discussions about money must be conducted in environments that minimize potential triggers, using communication methods that feel safe and comprehensible.

The fundamental goal transcends mere financial contribution; it's about constructing a supportive system that recognizes neurodivergent individuals' distinctive capabilities while providing a scaffolded pathway to independent economic management.

Parents evolve from traditional financial gatekeepers to strategic, empathetic guides—creating frameworks that respect individual neurological differences while offering robust, compassionate guidance. This approach demands exceptional flexibility, deep emotional intelligence, and a commitment to understanding each neurodivergent adult child's unique economic potential.

Success isn't measured by traditional metrics but by incremental growth, increased self-understanding, and the gradual development of financial confidence tailored to individual cognitive landscapes.

You're balancing love and tough love, support, and empowerment while keeping your retirement and sanity intact. This chapter isn't just about numbers—it's about values, boundaries, and setting the stage for mutual respect.

Financial independence is a gift you give your child—and yourself.

Chapter 6:

Practical Tips—Living Spaces and Building the Home You Want

Alright, your young adult decided to move back and your home is about to become part substitute dorm room, part career counseling center, and part crash course in how many pizza boxes one human can accumulate in a week.

But before you start browsing witness protection programs, just breathe. This chapter is your survival guide to sharing space with the people who once thought the floor was a perfectly good substitute for a hamper. We're talking about how to handle a 26-year-old's gaming setup that's threatening to overthrow your living room, or what to do when your neurodivergent daughter's creative organizing system looks suspiciously like organized chaos to everyone else.

Think of your home as a theater where everyone's still learning their lines. Your role? Part director, part stagehand, and occasional improv artist when things go off-script (and trust me, they will).

Whether you're housing a young professional who's saving for a down payment, supporting a child with unique developmental needs, or helping someone bounce back from life's curveballs, this chapter gives you the tools to create harmony without losing your sanity.

Because let's face it—the only thing harder than teaching a teenager to drive is teaching an adult child that dinner doesn't magically appear in the fridge.

Discussing Household Goals

You've called a "family meeting," and your 25-year-old just rolled their eyes so hard you're worried they'll strain something. But stick with me here—because setting household goals doesn't have to feel like a corporate retreat gone wrong.

- Timing matters. Skip the 7 a.m. Sunday ambush or the "we need to talk" text that sends everyone into panic mode. Maybe catch them when they're actually awake (somewhere between their second coffee and first TikTok scroll), and casually mention you'd like their input on making the house work better for everyone. Order pizza if you have to—bribery is totally fair game when you're trying to prevent World War III over whose turn it is to clean the microwave.

- Now, before you whip out that color-coded spreadsheet of chores (we see you, Type A parents), remember this isn't about recreating your 1992 house rules. Your adult child might actually have some solid ideas about sustainable living that don't involve your ancient paper towel addiction. Maybe they'll suggest a composting system that doesn't attract every raccoon in the zip code.

- The key? Make it a conversation, not a lecture. Sure, you need to address why their gym bag has become a permanent living room fixture, but they might have valid points about your habit of blasting Fox News at 6 a.m. Write everything down—not because you're keeping score, but because everyone's brain works differently. Your ADHD daughter might prefer a phone reminder app, while your son needs a whiteboard the size of Kansas.

- Speaking of different needs: If your child is neurodivergent, traditional chore charts might be as useful as a chocolate teapot. Instead, work with their strengths. Maybe your autistic son excels at organizing but struggles with time-sensitive tasks.

Perfect—he can manage the pantry while someone else handles the perishables.

- Create clear boundaries around shared spaces without turning your home into a military zone. Yes, the kitchen needs cleaning after midnight snacks, but maybe the "no shoes on the couch" rule from their teen years can retire along with your mom jeans.

This isn't about creating a perfect system—it's about building a framework flexible enough to bend without breaking. Your household agreement should be a living document, not tablets carved in stone. And sometimes the best solutions come from the most unexpected sources—like when your "lazy" kid suggests a brilliant digital chore-tracking app that actually works.

Chores: Dividing and Conquering

"So, who's doing the dishes tonight?" Cue the sudden epidemic of urgent phone calls, mysterious headaches, and the classic "I did them last time."

Hey, it's nothing new, it's the Olympic sport of chore avoidance, where your adult child could win gold in the "I'll do it later" marathon.

This is where you try convincing a 24-year-old that the dishwasher isn't actually a magical portal where dirty dishes disappear forever. But before you start dreaming about shipping them off to a monastery (where cleanliness is actually next to godliness), let's crack the code on making chores work in your multi-generational household.

- **Task-based assignments:** Think of it like a bizarre game show where contestants pick their poison. Your son might actually volunteer for bathroom duty because he can blast his music without judgment. Your daughter might claim the laundry because she doesn't trust anyone else with her "dry clean only" collection that mysteriously includes every t-shirt she owns.

- **Area-based assignments:** These work like real estate divisions, minus the property values. "This is my kingdom," declares your kid about the upstairs bathroom, right until they realize kingdoms need regular cleaning. Suddenly they're trying to negotiate a trade deal involving their car-washing skills and your vacuuming expertise.

- **The rota system:** This sounds great on paper—like communism or fat-free cheese. But it can work if you add some flexibility. Let everyone veto their kryptonite tasks. If your son would rather perform amateur dentistry than clean the microwave, let him swap for something equally annoying but less traumatic.

- **For your neurodivergent adult children:** We're not just rethinking the chores—we're redesigning the whole approach. That vacuum cleaner that sounds like a jet engine? Replace it with a quieter model. Those vague instructions to "tidy up"? Break them down like you're writing code: Step 1, Step 2, Step "no, the socks don't go in the fruit bowl."

- **Success tips:** Define "clean" like you're writing a legal document. "Doing the dishes" doesn't mean creating artistic towers of dirty plates or playing Jenga with coffee mugs. And please, for everyone's sanity, ban the phrase "I'll do it when I feel like it."

- **Tools matter:** That chore chart isn't just pretty wall art—it's your household's constitution. Make it flexible enough to accommodate real life (yes, sometimes work deadlines trump dusting), but firm enough to prevent your home from appearing on *Hoarders: Next Generation*.

Make chores meaningful without turning it into a lecture series on responsibility. Nobody wants to fold laundry, but everyone wants clean underwear. It's about connecting the dots between effort and outcome, like explaining that the mysterious fruit flies aren't actually your pet project.

Just also remember, perfect is the enemy of good enough. If your kid's idea of making their bed looks more like contemporary art than hospital corners, count it as a win. Because at the end of the day, a somewhat clean house with somewhat happy people beats a spotless house with murderous inhabitants.

Just keep the passive-aggressive sticky notes to a minimum.

Managing Shared Spaces

One minute you're admiring your carefully curated throw pillows, the next they've been repurposed as a fort for your daughter's impromptu work-from-home setup. And let's not even start on the kitchen counter that's morphed into a combination coffee bar, mail sorting facility, and impromptu TikTok studio.

Welcome to *Shared Space Survivor*, where the rules are made up and the boundaries keep disappearing. First things first: Let's get crystal clear about what's communal territory. The living room? Obviously shared (despite your son's attempt to claim squatter's rights with his gaming chair). The kitchen? A community zone, not a 24/7 pop-up restaurant where Mom magically appears to wash dishes. Now, here's where it gets tricky—dividing conquerable tasks from those requiring a hazmat suit. Indoor jobs might include ensuring the bathroom doesn't look like a Sephora exploded in it, while outdoor tasks cover everything from mowing the lawn to convincing your kid that their car isn't actually yard art.

But before you hand out assignments like a drill sergeant with a clipboard, consider this: some folks get overwhelmed faster than others. Your ADHD daughter might short-circuit at "organize the garage," but give her specific missions like "sort the recycling" or "clear the workbench," and suddenly she's Marie Kondo's apprentice.

The secret? Rotation.

Nobody wants to be permanently assigned to cat litter duty.

- Create a visual chart—think less kindergarten classroom, more Silicon Valley startup. Use a whiteboard, an app, or even interpretive dance signals, whatever works for your crew.

- Match tasks to strengths and schedules. Your night owl might prefer evening kitchen cleanup to morning garbage duty. Your early bird could handle breakfast dishes before their morning run.

The golden rule of shared spaces? "Leave it better than you found it." This means no, leaving empty coffee mugs around the house isn't an avant-garde art installation, and your laptop charging cable isn't a trip wire for unsuspecting family members. Create designated zones within common areas—a study corner in the living room, and a meal prep station in the kitchen that doesn't require archaeological excavation to find the cutting board. Think of it like urban planning.

Flexibility is key. Some days you'll nail it, with everyone flowing through shared spaces like a well-choreographed dance. Other days? It'll look more like a mosh pit at a heavy metal concert. That's okay—progress over perfection.

And for those moments when you find yourself staring at a sink full of dishes that are apparently invisible to everyone but you? Take a deep breath, remember that this too shall pass, and maybe invest in paper plates. Sometimes sanity is more important than sustainability.

Encouraging Time Management and Organization

"Just give me five more minutes!" Ah, the battle cry of the adult child who's been "about to start cleaning" since breakfast—yesterday's breakfast.

Time management with grown kids at home feels like trying to herd cats who have opposable thumbs and Instagram accounts. You've watched your son turn a 10-minute kitchen cleanup into a three-hour odyssey, complete with four snack breaks and an impromptu FaceTime session. Your daughter's "quick shower" somehow involves enough time to rewrite War and Peace. And don't get me started on their creative interpretation of "I'll do it first thing in the morning."

- Enter time blocking—the art of actually doing things when you say you'll do them. Novel concept, right? Break down the day like you're producing a Broadway show. For instance:

    - **9:00 a.m.:** Actually get out of bed (revolutionary, I know).

    - **9:30 a.m.:** Tackle that Mount Everest of laundry before it achieves sentience.

    - **10:00 a.m.:** Job hunt without falling into the TikTok void.

- For your neurodivergent young adults, think of time like a squirrely puppy—it needs structure to behave. Those timer apps aren't just fancy stopwatches; they're like training wheels for the brain. Twenty minutes of focused cleaning followed by ten minutes of whatever keeps them sane.

- And yes, some parents have discovered the magical motivating power of cold, hard cash. Call it a "household internship" if you must. Five bucks for a properly loaded dishwasher beats finding spoons in the potted plants. Cheaper than therapy and more effective than screaming into a pillow.

- Create a command center (fancy talk for a calendar on the fridge) where everyone can see what needs doing. Add checkboxes because, let's face it, the satisfaction of checking things off is sometimes the only thing getting us through the day.

- Build in buffer time for the inevitable "But I just saw something really important on YouTube" moments.

Rome wasn't built in a day, and your kid's time management skills won't be either. But with enough structure, you might just get them to remember that wet towels don't belong on wooden furniture before mold evolves into a new life form.

Dealing With Procrastination and Avoidance

Your adult child's job applications sit untouched on their laptop while they scroll through social media. Sound familiar? You're watching the clock tick away opportunities, fighting the urge to grab that laptop and fill out those applications yourself.

But here's what's really happening behind those endless scrolling sessions: Your child isn't lazy—they're likely terrified. Moving back home already feels like wearing a name tag that screams "FAILURE" (it's not, but try telling their anxiety that). Each incomplete task isn't just procrastination; it's a protective shield against potential disappointment. Remember when they were five and wouldn't jump into the pool until you counted to ten... fifteen times? Same kid, bigger pool. The difference? Now they're drowning in expectations—their own, yours, and society's Instagram-perfect highlight reel.

- "You're avoiding the job search because you're scared of rejection," you want to say. Instead, try: "Hey, what kind of company culture are you hoping to find?" Watch how their eyes light up describing their dream workplace. That's your opening—their motivation hiding behind the fear.

- Start small. That mountain of tasks? Turn it into molehills. Instead of "find a job," break it down: "Spend 30 minutes updating your LinkedIn profile." Celebrate these tiny victories like you did in their first steps. Because guess what? These are the first steps too—just in grown-up shoes.

- Give them space that feels truly theirs. Let them paint that awful accent wall they've been Pinterest-ing. When they feel at home rather than like a guest in a museum, watch how their initiative grows. They might even do their laundry without being asked. Maybe.

- Set SMART goals together, but make them bite-sized. "Apply to three jobs this week" beats "Figure out your entire career by Friday." Partner up on bigger tasks—not as their taskmaster, but as their ally. Nothing builds confidence like having someone in your corner who believes in you.

- When conflicts bubble up (and they will), breathe before speaking. "I noticed the dishes haven't been done" lands better than "Why can't you just...?" Remember, they're probably already playing their greatest hits of self-criticism on repeat.

- Most importantly, celebrate progress over perfection. Did they make one phone call instead of five? That's one more than yesterday. Are they still job hunting after ten rejections? That's resilience in action.

You're not just teaching them to overcome procrastination—you're showing them how to face fear, build confidence, and keep moving forward even when Netflix beckons. And sometimes, that means letting them figure out their own timeline, even if it makes your eye twitch.

The Tough Love Approach: When "Pretty Please" Isn't Cutting It

You've tried the gentle approach. You've had the heart-to-hearts. You've even left passive-aggressive sticky notes on the unwashed dishes. Now you're watching your adult child treat your home like an all-inclusive resort.

Time for tough love. Not the "you're grounded" variety (they'd probably enjoy being sent to their room anyway). We're talking about grown-up consequences for grown-up choices.

- Wi-Fi password changes might seem petty, but nothing motivates a job search like watching Netflix buffer eternally. "The internet's working fine in the local coffee shop," you mention, sliding over a job application. Amazing how many resumes can be sent when Instagram isn't an option.

- Hiring a cleaning service sounds extreme? Wait until they see that $100 deducted from their account for professional dishwashing. Suddenly, loading the dishwasher doesn't seem so arduous. It's not about the money—it's about connecting actions with consequences in the real world.

But here's the tricky part: Tough love without the "love" part is just being tough. Every boundary needs a bridge back. "Once these applications are sent, let's grab coffee and brainstorm interview strategies." See what happened there? Consequence, then collaboration. You're not running a boot camp—you're running a launch pad. The goal isn't to make their life harder; it's to make independence more appealing than dependence. Sometimes that means letting them feel just uncomfortable enough in their comfort zone to want to leave it.

And yes, they might sulk. They might call you mean. But someday—probably when they're enforcing their own boundaries—they'll thank you.

So here you are—your retirement plans temporarily shelved, your spare room de-spared, and your grocery bill looking like you're feeding a small army. But between the sighs and eye-rolls, something beautiful is happening: You're all growing up together.

Your home has transformed from a museum of their childhood into something far messier but infinitely more valuable: an incubator for adult relationships. Those awkward family dinners? They're slowly morphing into actual conversations. That tension over household rules? It's teaching everyone the art of compromise—even if someone still needs reminding that wet laundry can't live in the washing machine forever.

You're not just providing a roof—you're offering a safety net with a built-in coaching team.

Chapter 7:

Practical Tips—

Intimate Relationships

Remember when dating meant watching them drive off in your car, saying a quick prayer, and waiting up until curfew?

But now you're bumping into their significant other in the kitchen at 7 a.m., both of you awkwardly reaching for the coffee filters, pretending this is totally normal.

Reality check time: Your adult child's romantic life didn't press pause just because they moved back home. And while you might fantasize about instituting a "no closed doors" policy like it's 2010, you're not dealing with teenagers anymore. You're sharing space with grown adults who happen to share your DNA—and their relationships are as real as yours. The good news? You don't have to choose between feeling comfortable in your own home and supporting your child's emotional life. This isn't about picking between being the cool parent who pretends not to notice anything or the strict parent who treats their 25-year-old like they're 15.

There's a middle ground, and we're going to find it.

Think of it this way: You're not just setting house rules—you're creating a template for healthy relationships. How you handle this situation shows your child what respectful boundaries look like in practice. Plus, let's be honest: nothing speeds up the motivation to move out quite like having to check the family Google calendar before planning a date night.

Respecting Everyone's Comfort Level

You're settling in for your Sunday night TV ritual when mysterious giggles echo from upstairs. Time to crank up that volume!

Well, it's all part of the show—the delicate dance of hosting your adult child's love life. It's like running a bed and breakfast where the guests don't pay, and the entertainment isn't exactly PG-13.

- Let's start with the elephant in the room: overnight visitors. "But Mom, Sarah, and I have been dating for six months!" Sure, and your mortgage has been running for fifteen years. Time to channel your inner property manager. Weekend visits? Maybe. Tuesday night Netflix and chill? That's a hard pass. And please, no surprise sleepovers that leave everyone doing the awkward morning shuffle.

- Speaking of surprises, finding your child's latest Tinder match raiding your fridge at 2 a.m. isn't exactly what you meant by "making yourself at home." Save the random hookups for their future apartment. Your home isn't a revolving door for dating apps gone wild.

- Now, about those keys. Your daughter's boyfriend might be "practically family," but so is your cousin Jerry, and he doesn't have a spare key either. Unless there's a ring involved (and sometimes not even then), keep those keys close and your security system closer.

- "But I pay rent!" they protest, waving their monthly contribution like a golden ticket. Time for some real talk: "Sweetie, that $400 barely covers your share of the utilities, let alone gives you landlord privileges. Want to draft a formal lease agreement? Great! It'll include a lovely section about guest policies and eviction terms."

The key is setting these boundaries early—before you find yourself hiding in your own bedroom because someone's having a makeout session in the family room. Try this: "We love having Alex over, but we need a heads-up. Think of it like making a dinner reservation, except the dinner is free, and the dress code is 'please wear something.'"

Some helpful phrases to keep in your pocket:

- "This is still a family home, not a college dorm."

- "We respect your relationship, but we also respect our need for peace and quiet after 10 p.m."

- "Yes, your rent contribution is appreciated. No, it doesn't come with unlimited guest privileges."

Remember, you're not being unreasonable—you're being a homeowner who doesn't want to feel like an accidental voyeur in their own house. Besides, nothing says "time to get your own place" quite like having to text your parents before inviting your partner over.

And for those especially difficult conversations? Break out the rental listings. Sometimes a gentle reminder that independence comes with its own set of keys (and privacy) works wonders.

Because at the end of the day, everyone deserves to feel comfortable in their space—even if that space includes your adult child's blossoming romance.

Creating Space for Your Adult Child's Dating Life

You used to worry about them crossing the street safely. Now you're worrying about their Tinder safety settings. This whole parenting evolution thing is wild, isn't it?

Your role has shifted from playground supervisor to reluctant relationship roommate, and sometimes it feels like walking a tightrope while juggling everyone's emotions.

"Mom, I'm an adult!" they declare, while simultaneously asking if you can wash their lucky date-night shirt. Yes, they're adults—adults who still haven't figured out how to properly load a dishwasher. But when it comes to their romantic life, you're navigating new territory together.

Safety First

Let's talk safety first, because some conversations never get old, they just get more awkward. "Hey sweetie, I know you're excited about this new person, but could you share their last name and maybe their Instagram? You know, just in case you mysteriously disappear and I need to call the police." Frame it as basic safety protocol, not helicopter parenting gone rogue. It's about ensuring everyone's safety, even theirs.

For your neurodivergent young adults, dating comes with its own unique manual. Maybe they need extra processing time when discussing boundaries, or perhaps social cues around relationship etiquette feel like trying to read hieroglyphics. Skip the subtle hints and go straight for crystal clear communication: "Partners can visit between 2 p.m. and 10 p.m. on weekends" beats "Try to keep visits reasonable."

Boundaries and Communication

Now about those overnight guests—time to channel your inner diplomat. "We're happy to have Sarah stay over on weekends, but we need to know by Thursday so we can plan our own schedule."

Notice what happened there? You're not just setting boundaries; you're treating their relationship with respect while maintaining your sanity.

Sometimes they'll push back: "You never told me when you were having people over when I was a kid!" True, but you also paid the mortgage and didn't have to share a bathroom. Different roles, different rules.

Here's a script for those tricky conversations:

- "I respect your privacy, and I won't interrogate you about your dating life. But if someone's staying in our home, I need to know who they are. Think of it as basic home security, not nosiness."

- For particularly sensitive situations, try:
    - "I noticed Alex seems uncomfortable around family dinners. Is there something we should know about to make them feel more welcome?" This opens the door for communication without prying.

- And when things get messy (because they will), have your de-escalation tactics ready:
    - "I understand you're upset, but slamming doors won't change the house rules."
    - "Let's take a break and discuss this when we're both calmer."
    - "Would it help to write down what you think fair boundaries would look like?"

Create quiet zones and designated spaces where your child can retreat with their partner without feeling overwhelmed by family activity. Maybe the basement becomes their date night sanctuary—just install some good soundproofing first.

The golden rule? Treat their relationships as real, even if you're secretly counting down the days until they move out. That means no eye-rolling when they're going through their third breakup this year, and yes, actually learning their partner's name (even if you suspect they won't last until Christmas). Because here's the truth: How you handle their romantic life now sets the tone for your future relationship.

Until then, keep some noise-canceling headphones handy, perfect your "I didn't hear anything" poker face, and remember: This too shall pass.

Handling Breakups and Divorce

Remember when fixing their broken heart meant a Band-Aid, a cookie, and their favorite show? Well, now, there they are, wrapped in their old high school blanket, binge-watching their third terrible reality show of the day. The ice cream supply is dwindling, and you're pretty sure they haven't changed clothes since Tuesday.

Your parental instincts are screaming "Fix it!" But this isn't a scraped knee—it's a shattered relationship that even your famous chocolate chip cookies can't mend.

"I never want to date again!" they declare, while simultaneously scrolling through their ex's social media. You bite your tongue, resisting the urge to point out that stalking their ex's Instagram at 3 a.m. isn't exactly the path to healing. Instead, try: "I hear you. This really hurts. Want to talk about it while we walk the dog?" There, you validated their pain while sneakily getting them out of those three-day-old sweatpants. A breakup isn't just emotional chaos—it's a complete disruption of their carefully constructed world. Their Tuesday movie nights with their partner are gone. Their shared grocery shopping routine? Vanished. Time to break out the calendars and create new patterns: "Let's plan your week together. What about making Thursday our farmers' market day?"

But what about the ex who practically lived at your house? The one who knew the Wi-Fi password and had their own coffee mug?

Time for some gentle but firm boundaries: "I know Jake was like family, but right now, we need to give everyone space to heal. Maybe we can revisit this in a few months." And yes, you might need to change that Wi-Fi password finally.

Watch for the danger signs: excessive sleeping, skipping meals, or the dreaded "I'll just text them one more time." Your role? Part counselor, part boundary keeper, part reality checker. "Instead of sending that text, why don't we sign up for that pottery class you've been eyeing? Clay is very throwable."

For the especially tough days, have your support script ready:

- "No, you're not unlovable. You're going through a breakup while living with your parents—that would make anyone feel vulnerable."

- "Yes, it's okay to cry. No, it's not okay to drunk-dial them at midnight."

- "Of course, you can stay in today, but tomorrow we're getting you out of this room, even if it's just to check the mail."

And when they start dating again? Resist the urge to run background checks on their Hinge matches. Your job isn't to prevent future heartbreak—it's to be their safe landing spot when turbulence hits. This isn't just about surviving a breakup; it's about learning to process adult emotions while sharing space with the people who remember when you couldn't tie your own shoes. It's messy, it's complicated, and sometimes it means pretending you don't hear them crying in the shower.

Sometimes the best support you can offer is simply being there.

But here's the silver lining: This might be one of the last heartbreaks they navigate under your roof.

My Adult Child Is LGBTQ+: Love Doesn't Need a Renovation Permit

"Mom, Dad... Alex isn't just my roommate." There's that moment—the one where your child is watching your face like it's a final exam they're terrified of failing.

Your response? It matters more than those college tuition checks you wrote.

"Thank you for telling us. Now, does Alex still want to come for Sunday dinner? Because I need to know if they're vegetarian."

It's not uncommon to feel a mix of pride and uncertainty. On the one hand, you're amazed at your child's courage. Conversely, you might feel overwhelmed—concerned about how society will treat them or whether you'll navigate this new chapter correctly. Spoiler: You don't have to be perfect. You just have to be present.

For some parents, this revelation can trigger feelings of grief, even if you fully accept and love your child. That's because you're letting go of a deeply ingrained narrative, one society has conditioned you to hold onto. Recognize these feelings without guilt—they're normal. But don't get stuck there. Your child's journey isn't about your loss; it's about their self-discovery.

What do you, as a parent do, when the emotional terrain gets rough?

- **Process privately:** Your child has been processing this for a long time. Now it's your turn but do it away from them. Talk to a trusted friend, a therapist, or even a support group like PFLAG. These feelings are valid, but they aren't your child's burden to carry.

- **Educate yourself:** Feeling lost? Start learning. Ask your child for resources or do your own research. Knowing the right language, understanding their challenges, and unlearning old biases show you're not just supportive—you're invested.

- **Validate them, always:** When your child comes out, they're trusting you with a piece of themselves they may have hidden for years. Your job is to honor that trust. A simple "I'm so proud of you for sharing this with me" goes a long way.

Let's talk house rules because love is love, but somebody still needs to empty the dishwasher. Those overnight guest policies you crafted? They apply whether your son's boyfriend or your daughter's girlfriend is visiting. No special treatment—positive or negative. "Partners can visit until 10 p.m. on weeknights" means all partners, not just the ones who match your old assumptions. They're gay, not disabled.

Remember when you thought you had to childproof your home? Now it's time to prejudice-proof it. That means Aunt Martha might need a gentle reminder that her "traditional values" commentary isn't welcome at family dinners. Your home isn't just a physical shelter anymore—it's an emotional safe harbor where your child can bring their whole self, including their partner.

For your young adult LGBTQ+ child, navigating both their identity and relationships might feel like trying to solve a Rubik's cube in the dark. They're processing their own needs while dealing with society's expectations. Clear communication becomes your power: "Can you tell me how you'd like us to refer to your partner when we're with extended family?"

Some practical magic for your parental toolkit:

- "We love you, and we want to understand. Can you recommend some resources we should read?"

- "Your partner is always welcome here, just like everyone else's partners—as long as they follow the 'no feet on the coffee table' rule."

- "If anyone in this family gives you grief, they'll have to answer to me. Yes, you're still my child and I appreciate your courage and honesty."

Watch your language evolve. "Future spouse" replaces "future husband/wife." "Partner" slides naturally into conversation where "boyfriend/girlfriend" used to be. It's like learning any new language—awkward at first, but worth every stumble.

And when your child's partner comes over? Treat them like you'd treat any potential in-law. Their sexuality doesn't "magically" turn them into a different alien species.

For those tougher moments:

- "I might say the wrong thing sometimes, but I'm learning because I love you."

- "No, you don't need to tone it down for family events. They need to turn up their acceptance."

- "Your relationship is just as valid as your sister's."

Your young adult child trusted you enough to show you more of who they've always been. Your job? Keep being their parent, just with updated software.

Because at the end of the day, love under your roof isn't about gender, identity, or even those house rules you've carefully crafted. It's about creating a space where your child knows they're accepted and cherished, irrespective of their sexual preferences.

De-escalation Methods for Difficult Conversations

Remember when they were toddlers and you learned that matching their tantrum energy only created a louder tantrum? Same principle applies now, except instead of fighting over bedtime, you're debating why their partner can't do laundry at 3 a.m.

Now let's layer in the psychological toll this might take on you, the parent. Watching your child push back against house rules—or worse, accuse you of not understanding them—can feel like a personal attack. You're not just managing logistics here; you're grappling with the fear of losing your connection to them. It's tough. You're trying to maintain a functional, respectful home while nurturing a relationship with your young adult child. Every argument might feel like a high-stakes referendum on whether they see you as controlling, out-of-touch, or—gulp—unsupportive. The fear of "getting it wrong" can make you feel defensive, and their frustration might sting more than you expect.

Here's the thing: They're not questioning your love—they're questioning how that love translates into the rules and boundaries you're setting. It's okay to feel hurt, confused, or even angry, but don't let those emotions drive the conversation. Instead, focus on what's underneath: Both of you are trying to balance independence with connection.

- **Recognize the pattern:** If your first reaction is to dig your heels in or respond defensively, pause. What's the core issue? Usually, it's not just about laundry schedules—it's about feeling heard and respected.

- **Separate your feelings from the issue:** It's natural to feel unappreciated or misunderstood but don't let that derail the conversation. Instead of spiraling into "After everything I've done for you!", focus on solutions: "I need us to agree on quiet hours so I'm not woken up by the washing machine."

- **Find empathy amid the frustration:** Your adult child is also navigating big emotions—balancing their independence, relationships, and your expectations. A little compassion can go a long way: "I get that you're trying to juggle a lot. Let's figure out how to make this work for both of us."

Practical De-escalation Techniques

- Try this instead of "My house, my rules!" (which, let's face it, hasn't worked since they learned to roll their eyes): "I feel anxious when I wake up to unexpected guests in my kitchen. Can we work out a notification system that respects both our needs?" This way you're not the villain in their romance story—you're just someone who'd like to know they're there so you can wear pants when getting coffee.

- When they hit you with "You just don't understand modern relationships!" resist the urge to remind them about your own dating history. Instead: "You're right—things are different now. Help me understand what boundaries would work for everyone." Bonus points if you can say this without flashbacks to their teenage door-slamming phase.

- The secret? Timing. If they're already late for work and stressed about a presentation, maybe there are better moments to discuss their partner's tendency to use all the hot water. Wait for a calm moment, perhaps over those leftovers they haven't eaten yet: "Hey, while you're enjoying my lasagna, can we talk about morning shower schedules?" Sometimes emotions run hotter than that laptop they leave charging. That's your cue to press pause: "This conversation matters too much to have it while we're both frustrated. Let's grab coffee tomorrow and try again." Translation: "Please stop yelling about relationship rights while I'm trying to watch my show."

These conversations aren't really about overnight guests or relationship rules—they're about adults learning to share space while respecting each other's boundaries. And sometimes that means taking a deep breath, counting to ten, and remembering that you both want the same thing: peace.

So here you are, running an accidental bed and breakfast for your adult child's love life. The bathroom schedule looks like an air traffic control diagram, and you've mastered the art of perfectly timed coughing to announce your presence in hallways. But guess what? You're all surviving.

Remember when you thought teaching them about the birds and the bees was awkward? Now you're navigating morning-after-breakfast encounters and pretending you didn't notice their partner's car still parked outside at 7 a.m. But in this chaos, something beautiful is happening: You're all learning to dance in smaller spaces without stepping on each other's toes (mostly). Your home has become a living laboratory for relationship dynamics. Under your roof, they're learning how to balance love with responsibility and passion with practicality. And you? You're discovering that being a parent to an adult in love means knowing when to hold firm on boundaries and when to suddenly become very interested in gardening while they say goodnight on the porch.

Someday, they'll have their own space where they can make their own rules about overnight guests and breakfast protocols. Until then, keep the coffee strong, the boundaries clear, and your sense of humor stronger.

Chapter 8:

Practical Tips—Positive Mindset and Mental Wellness

Here you are, hiding in your walk-in closet at 10 p.m., stress-eating the emergency chocolate stash you cleverly hid behind your winter sweaters. Why? Because downstairs, your 26-year-old daughter is having her third existential crisis of the week about her career path, and your 24-year-old son hasn't left his room in two days because his startup idea got rejected.

This is the emotional roller coaster of hosting your adult children's quarter-life crises under your roof.

One minute you're celebrating their job interview success with a family dinner; the next, you're wondering if that meditation app you downloaded is actually working or if you just fell asleep during the "mindful breathing" session.

Some days, you're everyone's therapist: "Can we talk?" (Translation: "Can I monologue about my problems while you nod sympathetically and refill my coffee?") Other days, you're the villain in their story because you suggested, just maybe, that playing video games until 3 a.m. might not be the best coping mechanism for job search anxiety.

Experts talk about empty nest syndrome, but nobody warned you about full-nest-again syndrome—that special brand of chaos where your retirement fund, your son's depression, your daughter's anxiety, and the household's dwindling toilet paper supply all compete for your attention.

This chapter isn't just about surviving the emotional tsunami of multi-generational adult living. It's about thriving in it. Somewhere between your midnight closet chocolate sessions and their morning mood swings lies a sweet spot where everyone's mental health can coexist. Think of your home as an emotional greenhouse. With the right care and environment, everyone can grow. But keeping this greenhouse thriving means figuring out how to nurture your own emotional plants while helping them tend to theirs.

And yes, that often means learning to say, "I love you, but I need to put on my own oxygen mask first" without feeling guilty for taking a mental health day from being everyone's emotional support human.

The Elephant in Your Living Room:
Mental Health Matters

Your kid's back home, and something's off. Maybe they're sleeping until 3 p.m. or their room's starting to smell like teen spirit—but not the nostalgic kind. Your parental spider-sense is tingling, but this isn't like the time they were sixteen and "borrowed" the car for a joyride.

Adult mental health issues are trickier to spot; they show up dressed in business casual, carrying an air of "I'm fine" while subtly painting warning signs across their daily routines.

This isn't just about a bad day or a rough week. It's about those persistent patterns that quietly wave red flags, not one-off behaviors that can be brushed aside. Your parental instincts might whisper "something's not right," but mental health concerns require more than gut reactions—they need awareness, understanding, and a game plan that goes beyond grounding or a stern talk.

To start, focus on what you're observing. Are they withdrawing from friends they used to laugh with for hours? Are Netflix binges replacing meals? Is their job hunt full of big promises but no follow-through? This isn't laziness or rebellion—it's potentially a signal for help, masked by the complexities of adulthood. Educating yourself about common mental health struggles like anxiety, depression, or even burnout can make all the difference. You'll avoid the all-too-easy trap of jumping to conclusions and instead approach the conversation armed with insight and compassion.

It's tough—your first instinct might be to fix things, to offer solutions faster than they can finish explaining the problem. But addressing adult mental health isn't about quick fixes; it's about digging deeper, observing without judgment, and creating a safe space where they feel seen and supported.

Remember, the goal isn't to pry or play detective. It's about building trust and opening doors to conversations they may not even realize they need.

Sometimes, the hardest step isn't solving the problem—it's admitting there's one in the first place.

- **Your First Line of Defense: The Not-So-Obvious Signs**

Remember how you could tell they were lying about homework by that little eye twitch? Well, mental health red flags are sneakier.

Sure, there's the classic "I'm fine" while wearing the same sweatpants for a week straight. But watch for the subtle stuff: empty promises about job applications, ghosting their friends, or treating their bedroom like a fallout shelter.

When their Instagram-worthy breakfast sits untouched, or they've memorized every Netflix category (including "Critically-acclaimed Experimental Puppet Shows"), it's time to pay attention. These aren't just quirky millennial traits—they're potential distress signals. Document what you notice—changes in mood, habits, or routines—so you can bring it up without sounding accusatory.

Be aware of:

    o **Mood swings:** Sudden shifts between happiness, anger, or apathy.

- **Sleep disturbances:** Excessive sleeping or insomnia.
- **Changes in appetite:** Overeating or lack of appetite.
- **Energy levels:** Chronic fatigue or hyperactivity.
- **Difficulty concentrating:** Forgetfulness or inability to focus.
- **Social withdrawal:** Avoiding family and friends.
- **Hygiene neglect:** Unkempt appearance or ignoring personal care.
- **Substance use:** Increased reliance on alcohol, drugs, or medication.
- **Physical symptoms:** Frequent headaches, stomachaches, or muscle tension.
- **Avoidance behaviors:** Refusing to engage in activities they once enjoyed.
- **Declining performance:** Struggling with work, studies, or household responsibilities.
- **Emotional dysregulation:** Overreacting to minor stressors or triggers.
- **Passive language:** Frequent use of "I can't" or "What's the point?"
- **Technology dependency:** Excessive time online or gaming as escapism.
- **Financial irresponsibility:** Overspending or ignoring bills and obligations.
- **Guilt or worthlessness:** Statements like "I'm a burden" or "I can't do anything right."

- **Playing Coach, Not Referee**

"Just snap out of it!" works about as well as telling a fish to ride a bicycle. Instead, try this: When they're spiraling about their third failed job interview, help them spot the plot holes in their "I'm utterly unemployable" story. "Remember when you organized that charity event? Pretty sure unemployable people don't raise $5,000 for homeless pets."

Use specific examples to challenge negative thinking. It's harder to argue with evidence of their strengths.

Be aware of:

- **Defensiveness:** Resistance to feedback or advice.
- **Black-and-white thinking:** Viewing situations as all good or all bad.
- **Negative self-talk:** Harsh criticism of their abilities or worth.
- **Avoiding accountability:** Blaming others or circumstances for problems.
- **Fear of failure:** Avoiding opportunities to prevent disappointment.

- **The Fine Art of Listening**

Your parental toolbox probably includes a PhD in advice-giving. Time to earn a master's in zipping it. When they're venting about their quarter-life crisis, resist the urge to solve everything. Sometimes "That sounds really tough" beats your TED talk on resilience.

Set aside time to listen without distractions. Phones down, Netflix paused—it shows you're fully present.

Be aware of:

- **Suppressed emotions:** Hesitation to share feelings or thoughts.

- **Signs of overwhelm:** Struggling to articulate concerns or breaking down when discussing issues.

- **Mismatched words and actions:** Saying "I'm fine" while displaying visible distress.

- **Disconnection:** Using humor or sarcasm to deflect deeper conversations.

- **The Support Squad: It Takes a Village (and Maybe a Therapist)**

You're good, but you're not that good. Sometimes professional help isn't just a good idea—it's as necessary as that coffee maker you can't live without.

Frame therapy like a personal trainer for their brain, not a last resort for "crazy people." Bonus points if you normalize it: "Yeah, I talked to someone after my divorce. Best money I ever spent on my mental health."

Be aware of:

- **Therapy stigma:** Fear of judgment or misunderstanding about mental health care.

- **Reluctance to seek help:** Dismissing the need for professional intervention.

- **Financial barriers:** Inability to afford therapy or medication.

- **Misinformation:** Belief in myths like "therapy is only for extreme cases."

- **Co-occurring issues:** Undiagnosed neurodivergence, trauma, or chronic illness.

- Walking the Tightrope: Independence vs. Support

Here's the tricky part: balancing between helicopter parent and absentee landlord. Too much hovering, and you'll suffocate them. Too hands-off, and they might start thinking the dryer lint is a food group. Find that sweet spot where you're available but not overwhelming.

The Golden Rules of Mental Health Support

- Drop the fix-it mentality faster than your attempts at TikTok dances
- Keep your door open
- Watch for progress, not perfection
- **Remember:** Your role is wingman, not pilot

Your home's become a halfway house between their old life and whatever comes next. Make it a pit stop where they can refuel their mental health tank without feeling like they're sixteen again. Because let's face it—nobody wants to relive those years, especially not with a fully developed frontal lobe and a student loan payment.

Supporting your adult child's mental health isn't about having all the answers. It's about creating space where questions don't feel like failure and help doesn't feel like weakness.

Narcissism 101

Now, let's talk about what I fondly call the "Me, Myself, and I" syndrome. Narcissistic behaviors aren't just eye rolls and dramatic sighs. They're a full-contact sport where your feelings are the punching bag, and logic takes a permanent vacation.

Your adult child doesn't just want the spotlight—they want the entire theater, the marquee, and possibly your retirement savings to fund their one-person show with cherries on top. It's exhausting, disorienting, and sometimes outright heartbreaking.

Let's unpack the red flags, psychological toll, and survival tips.

The Gaslighting Gambit: When Reality Becomes Optional

Gaslighting is like emotional jazz—improvisation where your reality gets rewritten faster than you can say "That's not what happened." Suddenly, that argument you distinctly remember? Nope. You're "misremembering." That promise they made? Clearly, you misunderstood. Welcome to the twilight zone of family dynamics.

Keep an eye out for:

- rewriting past events
- minimizing your feelings
- blame shifting

How to cope:

- Keep notes on important conversations. You're not being paranoid—you need to document everything.

- If something feels off, it probably is. Don't let them overwrite your instincts.

- Avoid engaging in debates about "what really happened." Stick to facts and move forward.

Boundary Boot Camp: Your Survival Guide

Narcissistic kids don't respect boundaries; they test them, push them, and try to obliterate them. When your darling narcissist tries to push past your limits, stand firm. Not with anger, but with the calm certainty of someone who's survived toddler tantrums and teenage rebellion.

Your new mantra? "No" is a complete sentence. No explanations. No justifications. Just. No.

Expect tantrums, guilt trips, and drama. Stay calm—they thrive on emotional reactions. It might be tough, sort of like trying to stop a tornado with kitchen towels, but just stick to it. Why? Because you're not just sticking to your word, you're building a steel curtain of respect.

You don't need to play this game.

The Empathy Workout: Building Emotional Muscles

Here's a radical thought (I have plenty of those): Your self-absorbed offspring might not be a lost cause. They're like emotional toddlers in adult bodies—needing guidance, but not infantilization. Encourage them to see beyond their reflection.

- Ask questions that make them step outside their personal echo chamber—"How would the world look if everyone treated others exactly like you do?" Boom. Mental push-ups for the ego.

- Use relatable examples—"Imagine if your boss treated you like that."

- Highlight inconsistencies between their words and actions without shaming them.

The Social Connection Prescription

Narcissists are "allergic" to genuine connection because their interactions revolve around self-interest. So, prescribe a healthy dose of real-world interaction. Volunteer work, team sports, group activities—anything that requires them to consider someone else's oxygen needs. It's like emotional cross-training. And be sure to limit screen time. Excessive social media fuels their self-absorption and comparison traps.

The Manipulation Playbook: Recognize and Deflect

Guilt trips are their favorite frequent flyer miles. They'll weaponize emotions faster than you can say "But I'm your mother." Your response? Calm. Consistent. Unshakeable.

Master these counter-moves:

- **Detach emotionally:** Stay calm and neutral, even if they escalate.

- **Use scripted responses:** "I understand you're upset, but this is my decision" can shut down arguments.

- **Spot the patterns:** If every conversation feels like a chess game where you're always in checkmate, it's manipulation.

If your interactions feel more like a toxic relationship than a parent-child dynamic, something's wrong. Keep your eyes peeled for the following red flags:

- **Excessive control:** They dictate your time, money, or emotional energy.

- **Emotional whiplash:** One moment they're charming; the next, they're critical or cruel.

- **Walking on eggshells:** You're constantly second guessing yourself to avoid triggering them.

Natural Consequences: The Universe's Report Card

Stop being their get-out-of-jail-free card. Narcissism thrives on dependency; independence is the antidote. When they mess up, let them feel the heat. Lost job? Help them polish the resume, but don't call your golf buddy for a pity placement. Forgot to pay rent? Welcome to the magical world of late fees. Let life teach them what boundaries can't.

Confronting narcissistic behaviors isn't about proving you're right. It's about creating space for genuine connection. Some days, that means holding the line. Other days, it means holding space.

Your adult child isn't a project to fix—they're a deeply flawed human, just like the rest of us, learning to navigate a world that doesn't revolve around them. The difference? Their flaws might burn you out if you're not careful. Your job? Be the lighthouse, not the rescue boat. You're not responsible for their happiness.

Protect your peace, lead with compassion, and remember: boundaries are love, too.

The Velcro Dilemma: Addressing Emotional Dependence

So, you've accidentally created an emotional dependency masterpiece where your adult child has mastered the art of turning you into a human Swiss Army knife—part therapist, part ATM, part life coach.

Think your kid's attachment style is intense? Imagine a koala bear with abandonment issues and a graduate degree. They've got more emotional baggage than an airport lost and found, and you're their favorite luggage cart.

Let's call this exercise "Soft Skills, Hard Truths."

Your mission: Transform your adult child from a human remora into a functional, somewhat independent creature.

- Step one? Stop being their human GPS for life decisions. When they call you to decide between red or blue socks, it's time for an intervention. Not the dramatic TV kind—the "I believe in you" kind that gradually turns them into a decision-making ninja.

- Encourage them to weigh options by asking, "What do you think makes the most sense here?" Redirect questions back to them instead of giving quick solutions.

- Provide tools, not answers. Suggest decision-making frameworks or resources like budgeting apps, job boards, or even a good old pros-and-cons list.

- Setting boundaries isn't about building walls. It's about creating windows. Show them you trust their capabilities more than they trust themselves. "I know you'll figure this out" becomes your emotional WD-40, lubricating their independence mechanism.

  - Be clear on what you're stepping back from. Instead of "I can't help you right now," try, "I won't be involved in managing your finances anymore, but I'm happy to recommend resources."

  - Reinforce the boundary gently but consistently when tested. "I trust you to handle this" isn't just encouragement—it's a reminder that you're serious about the shift.

- Model independence. Take classes. Pursue hobbies. Have friendships that don't involve discussing your child's latest drama. Show them adulting isn't a punishment—it's a choose-your-own-adventure book.

  - Share your experiences casually: "I've started doing yoga—it's been great for my focus!" This shows them that personal growth doesn't stop at adulthood.

  - Set boundaries for emotional availability: "I'm stepping out for a movie tonight, let's chat tomorrow." It demonstrates that your life isn't on hold for their crises.

- Create a road map where you're gradually demoted from mission control to occasional satellite check-in. Start small: budget planning, apartment hunting, career exploring. Your role? Cheerleader, not player-manager.
    - Use milestones as checkpoints: "Why don't you find a few apartments to consider? I'll help you look over your top two choices."
    - Make their independence a shared goal: "How about we work toward you handling all your bill payments by the end of this year?"

Every time you resist solving their problem, you're basically emotional weightlifting. They might wobble. They might whine. But slowly, they're building those self-reliance muscles. Your goal isn't perfection. It's progress. If they manage to schedule a dentist appointment without three panic-stricken phone calls to you, throw a mental parade.

Emotional dependence isn't a life sentence. It's a phase—like their questionable fashion choices or that time they thought energy drinks were a food group. You're raising an adult who calls you because they want to, not because they can't breathe without your input. Someone who sees you as a trusted advisor, not a human safety net.

Neurodivergence: The Brain's Scenic Route

You can think of this as parenting's advanced difficulty level—where the instruction manual was written in a language nobody quite understands, looking more like abstract art than navigation.

Your neurodivergent adult child's brain isn't broken. It's just wired differently—like a Ferrari running on a completely unique operating system. Normal rules? They're more like suggestions. Communication? Think diplomatic translation service. This isn't about accommodating. It's about celebrating a different kind of brilliance. Your neurodivergent adult child isn't a project. They're a masterpiece in progress, drawing outside society's lines.

Your home becomes a research lab of understanding. Experiment with communication. Learn their language. Discover what makes their neurons dance with joy.

- Forget flowery language. Neurodivergent brains love precision like mathematicians love clean equations. "Clean the house" might as well be "Solve world hunger." Break. It. Down. "Put dirty dishes in dishwasher" beats "tidy up" every single time.

- Sensory sensitivity isn't drama. It's their nervous system's personal security system. Loud noises? Potential threat. Scratchy sweater? Psychological warfare. Your mission: Create a sanctuary that feels safe, not suffocating.

- Think of a comfort kit as a survival pack for their nervous system. Noise-canceling headphones? Check. A weighted blanket that feels like a constant, gentle hug? Double-check. Soft lighting that doesn't scream "interrogation room"? Triple-check.

- Color-coded schedules aren't just cute—they're lifelines. Red for urgent. Blue for flexibility. Green for "this can wait." Suddenly, chaos transforms into a comprehensible landscape.

Neurodivergence isn't a puzzle to solve. It's a perspective to understand. Your adult child sees the world through a kaleidoscope while everyone else uses a standard lens. Fascinating? Absolutely. Challenging? You bet.

Stop trying to "fix" them. Start celebrating their unique brain wiring. They might need extra support navigating social situations but possess creativity that'll make your jaw drop.

Surviving the Emotional Thunderstorm

Stress is like the uninvited houseguest of life—it shows up unannounced, overstays its welcome, and leaves chaos in its wake.

Whether it's a work deadline breathing down your neck, relationship drama that could rival a reality TV show, or the simple joy of realizing your car needs repairs *again*, stress has a way of finding you.

Living together means stress isn't just your problem—it's a family reunion nobody requested.

You might find yourself where your home is like an emotional pressure cooker where anxiety simmers faster than instant ramen. Your adult child might be broadcasting stress signals stronger than your Wi-Fi, and you're about to become the household's emotional first responder.

What to do?

- Seriously. *Breathe.* Anxiety loves dramatic entrances. Your job? Become the bouncer. Box breathing isn't just for Navy SEALs—it's for anyone who's ever felt like screaming into a throw pillow. Four counts in, four counts hold, four counts out, four counts pause. Repeat until you're not plotting elaborate escape routes. It's like a reset button for your nervous system.

- Exercise isn't punishment. It's your brain's secret weapon. A walk isn't just walking—it's telling anxiety, "Not today." Even a 10-minute walk can work wonders on your mood—movement is medicine.

    o **Pro tip:** Those free YouTube fitness videos? Your new family therapy. Nothing bonds like collective awkward stretching and mild sweating.

- Carve out a space where stress goes to die. Think soft lighting, noise-canceling vibes, and maybe a chair so comfortable it should require a medical prescription. This isn't just a room—it's an emotional Switzerland. Neutral. Peaceful. Non-negotiable. Imagine everyone simultaneously taking a collective chill pill. One hour. No phones. No drama. Just pure, unadulterated relaxation. Reading. Meditation. Staring blankly. Whatever resets your internal chaos meter. Calm and Headspace are great mindfulness apps, like personal Zen masters living in your phone. Ten minutes of guided meditation might be the difference between a functioning human and a total meltdown.

- Stress snacks might feel like a hug from the inside, but a diet of chips and ice cream won't do you any favors long-term. Fuel your body with balanced meals and throw in a leafy green or two.

- Overcommitting is a one-way ticket to Stressville. Learn to say no without guilt. Remember, "I don't have the capacity for that right now" is a full sentence.

- Surround yourself with friends who lift you up, not ones who drain your energy. A strong support network is like an emotional umbrella—you don't want to face storms without it.

- Stress loves sleep-deprived brains because they're easier to rattle. Aim for 7–9 hours of quality sleep, and no, doom-scrolling in bed doesn't count as "winding down." If you struggle with racing thoughts, try journaling before bed. Dumping your worries onto paper can clear your mind and make space for actual rest.

- If stress starts feeling like quicksand you can't escape, don't tough it out alone. Therapy isn't a sign of weakness—it's like hiring a guide to help you navigate the storm.

Speaking of dumping worries, here are a couple of other quick tips when you find yourself in the midst of a stress storm:

- Grab a notebook and spill your thoughts onto the page. The goal is to get the chaos out of your head and onto paper.

- Step away, even if it's just for five minutes. Go outside, make a cup of tea, or stare at a plant. Sometimes the best way to manage stress is to pause (and breathe, of course).

- Phone a friend. Talking to someone who gets you can be like opening an emotional pressure valve.

- Watch a funny video, listen to a comedy podcast, or remember that time you tripped in public and tried to play it cool. Laughter is the ultimate stress antidote.

Your home isn't just a living space. It's an emotional training ground where everyone learns to surf life's crazy waves without wiping out. Survival is about showing up, breathing through the chaos, and occasionally eating ice cream straight from the container.

Remember, stress might be unavoidable, but being consumed by it isn't. You're stronger than the storm, and every time you face it head-on, you prove it.

The Nocturnal Nightmare: Enough Sleep

Your adult child's sleep schedule? Highly likely that it's more unpredictable than a cat on espresso.

Remember when you could control bedtimes? Adorable. Now you're living with a human who treats sunrise like a mythical concept and 3 a.m. as prime productivity hours.

- **Why Sleep Is Mission-Critical for Mental Wellness**

Let's pause here for a reality check: Sleep isn't just about recharging the body. It's the janitor for the mind, sweeping away mental clutter, improving memory, and keeping emotions from spiraling into chaos. Chronic sleep deprivation is like giving anxiety and irritability a free pass to set up camp in your brain. It reduces your ability to concentrate, makes decision-making harder, and even dampens emotional resilience—something everyone could use more of, especially in a shared household.

When your adult kid treats sleep as optional, they're not just messing with their mood; they're jeopardizing their mental health and yours. A well-rested brain is better at handling stress, fostering creativity, and navigating life's inevitable curveballs.

- **The Noise Negotiation Treaty**

Quiet hours aren't a suggestion—they're a survival strategy. Think of it like international diplomacy, but with fewer suits and more sleep masks. "I need silence between 10 p.m. and 6 a.m." becomes your constitutional amendment. By maintaining quiet hours, you're safeguarding not just your sleep but your ability to function like a semi-civilized human being.

- **Sleep Hygiene: Not Just a Fancy Term**

Turns out, "go to bed" isn't sophisticated advice for your nocturnal offspring. We're talking strategic sleep optimization.

    o Reduce caffeine? Check.

    o Put down the smartphone? Negotiable, but strongly recommended.

    o Create a wind-down ritual that doesn't involve blue screens? Absolutely revolutionary.

Encouraging healthy sleep habits isn't about being a nag; it's about helping your kid prioritize their mental well-being. Sleep hygiene isn't just fluff—it's the foundation for clearer thinking, better emotional regulation, and even physical health. And yes, that means pointing out that falling asleep to TikTok videos isn't exactly the same as meditative breathing.

- **Chore Tetris: Scheduling for Sanity**

When your kid's awake hours look like a randomized spreadsheet, chores become a creative challenge. Night owl doing dishes at 2 a.m.? Fine. Early bird handling morning laundry? Perfect. The goal? Household harmony without military-level scheduling.

Sleep chaos doesn't have to derail shared responsibilities. Think of chore assignments as an adaptive strategy—a way to keep the peace and keep things clean, no matter whose internal clock is ticking.

- **The Compromise Waltz**

This isn't about winning. It's about coexisting without plotting mutual destruction. Some nights, they'll be loud. Some mornings, you'll be cranky. The secret? Communicate like reasonable humans who occasionally inhabit different time zones.

Remind them that sleep isn't just personal—it's communal. Their 3 a.m. movie marathon could be your 7 a.m. zombie shuffle. Meeting in the middle ensures everyone gets at least a semblance of rest and sanity.

  - **Survival Toolkit**
    - Noise-canceling headphones
    - Flexible expectations
    - A sense of humor
    - Possibly wine (for you, not them)

Your adult child's sleep schedule is less a problem to solve and more a puzzle to navigate. Some days you'll be the Zen master of patience. On other days, you'll fantasize about soundproof rooms.

Substance Abuse: Navigating the Minefield of Addiction

This is where love meets tough love, and your living room becomes ground zero for the most challenging conversation of your parenting career. Substance abuse isn't just a problem—it's a really tough hustle nobody ever willingly signs up for.

Your adult child isn't a statistic. They're a human wrestling with a beast that's bigger than both of you. And you? You're about to take on the roles of counselor, peacekeeper, and emotional strategist all rolled into one.

The Warning Sign Decoder Ring

Addiction doesn't announce itself with a megaphone. It whispers through mood swings, late-night secrecy, and erratic behavior. Those unexplained cash withdrawals? The sudden interest in "privacy"? Red flags.

Signs to keep your eyes peeled for include:

- **Erratic behavior:** Sudden, unpredictable mood swings or reactions that seem out of character.

- **Secrecy:** Increased need for privacy, such as locking doors, hiding phones, or avoiding direct conversations.

- **Unexplained financial issues:** Frequent cash withdrawals, missing money, or valuables disappearing from your home.

- **Changes in social circles:** New friends who seem secretive or avoid family interactions, or a sudden withdrawal from long-term friendships.

- **Neglecting responsibilities:** Skipping work, school, or personal commitments without clear explanations.

- **Physical symptoms:** Bloodshot eyes, unexplained weight loss or gain, or unusual fatigue.

- **Changes in appearance:** Neglect of personal hygiene or noticeable shifts in how they dress and present themselves.

- **Sleep pattern disturbances:** Staying awake all night and sleeping through the day, or showing constant exhaustion.

- **Paranoia or defensiveness:** Overreacting to questions or acting suspiciously, as if they're always on edge.

- **Substance-related items:** Finding paraphernalia like empty pill bottles, rolling papers, or burnt foil.

But decoding these signs requires sharp observation, not judgment. Addiction often hides behind layers of denial—not just theirs, but sometimes yours, too. It's easy to dismiss odd behaviors as "just a phase." However, the quicker you catch these signals, the sooner you can step in.

Just always remember that you're not a detective solving a crime—you're a parent trying to understand and support.

The Conversation

Confronting substance abuse is like defusing an emotional bomb. One wrong word and everything explodes. "I'm worried" beats "You're destroying your life" every single time.

Approach with the gentleness of a therapist and the backbone of a drill sergeant.

Start with concern, not accusations. Instead of saying, "Why are you doing this to yourself?" try, "I've noticed some changes, and I'm really concerned about you." This opens a door instead of slamming it shut. Expect defensiveness. Expect denial. But stay steady. The goal isn't to win an argument; it's to plant a seed of awareness that could grow into a willingness to seek help.

With that said, communicate boundaries in this regard as clear as daylight. Your home isn't a free-for-all addiction playground. "No substances" isn't a suggestion—it's your household constitution. Think of it like a non-negotiable peace treaty. Violate the terms? Consequences activate. Boundaries are your lifeline. They protect you, your family, and even your adult child from the chaos addiction brings. Enforcing these limits isn't cruelty; it's clarity. Make your rules firm but fair: "I love you, but I can't allow your choices to destroy this household." Consistency is key. If your child sees you waver, the boundary becomes meaningless. Stand firm, even when it's hard—especially when it's hard.

Lastly, remember our little chat about sleep? For your adult child, poor sleep only fuels the addiction cycle. Sleep deprivation amplifies cravings, weakens impulse control, and disrupts the emotional regulation they desperately need to overcome this battle. Encourage healthy sleep habits for them while prioritizing your own rest. Think of sleep as your mental armor—without it, you're fighting unprotected.

The Support Playbook

Offering help isn't a weakness. It's your superpower—rehab resources, counseling contacts, support group information—it's all important for recovery. But—and this is crucial—you can't drag them to recovery. You can only illuminate the path and:

- keep loving them

- hate the addiction

- don't become their enabler

- stay sane

The reality of addiction recovery is that some days, they'll take one step forward. Other days, they'll sprint backward. Stay consistent. Be the lighthouse, not the rescue boat. Show up. Set boundaries. Repeat.

Substance abuse turns your home into an emotional war zone. But here's the secret: You're stronger than you think. More resilient than the addiction. More hopeful than the darkest moment.

You're not alone. You're not failing. You're fighting the hardest, most loving battle of your life.

Your home isn't just a living space. It's a complex emotional laboratory where everyone's experimenting with adulting. Some experiments will fail spectacularly. Others might surprise you.

When tensions rise faster than your blood pressure, your magic phrase becomes, "Let's pause and come back when we're not auditioning for a reality TV showdown." Think of de-escalation as emotional judo to help maintain the collective emotional and mental well-being of your household. You're not surrendering. You're strategically stepping back to preserve the relationship—and your remaining hair follicles.

You're not just a parent. You're a diplomat, therapist, and occasional comedic relief. Some days, you'll feel like you're winning.

Just keep in mind, that rigid expectations are emotional quicksand. The more you struggle, the deeper you sink. Adapt. Breathe. Remember: This is a phase, not a life sentence.

Chapter 9:

Simple But Effective Self-Care Habits for Parents

You've just Marie Kondo'd the kids' bedrooms, ordered champagne, and started planning those romantic weekend getaways. Freedom was your new best friend, and retirement looked sexier than your wedding day.

Then *voila* (in a perfect French accent)! Your adult child arrives.

Ha! It's the midlife plot twist—from empty nest to full house, again. You have come full circle! Shall we high-five?

Remember how you spent two decades fantasizing about quiet mornings and uninterrupted coffee? How you dreamed of spontaneous date nights and bathroom time that didn't involve negotiating shower schedules? The universe just served you a grande-sized cup of "Just Kidding!" One minute you're browsing travel brochures, the next you're restocking the pantry like you're preparing for a small army invasion.

This isn't just about sharing space. It's a full-blown identity crisis wrapped in familial love and mild panic. Your meticulously planned "me time" now competes with laundry negotiations and midnight kitchen raids. Your romantic dinners might involve your adult child's unexpected appearance, complete with takeout and life crisis du jour.

Turns out, you're part of a massive underground movement—here we are, trading war stories and survival strategies.

Look, it's not about loss. It's about rediscovering your relationship through an adult lens. Your child isn't a teenager anymore. They're a complex human navigating life's most turbulent decade.

Some days, you'll feel like a superhero. On other days, you'll wonder if witness protection might be a viable retirement plan. It's complicated and beautiful. It's a modern family adventure. Some moments will test every ounce of your patience. Others will surprise you with unexpected connection, laughter, and love so deep it'll make your previous empty nest dreams look like amateur hour.

Well, this is the Full House Revolution. Population: You, your adult child, and approximately 837 unresolved emotions.

The trick?

Don't lose yourself amidst all the fun!

The Freedom Heist

Ah, freedom—that magical concept where pajamas were optional, coffee stayed hot, and bathroom time didn't require a negotiation treaty?

Well, what can I say? Welcome to the new reality—where personal space is a mythical concept and "alone time" sounds like a foreign language.

Suddenly, wandering from bedroom to kitchen requires tactical planning. No more carefree morning struts in that ratty bathrobe you've loved for decades. Now, you're performing elaborate costume changes worthy of a Broadway production. One wrong turn, and you're giving an unintended morning show. Quiet reading? Ha! More like occasional paragraph consumption between life updates, random YouTube video shares, and unexpected emotional downloads. Your carefully curated reading nook has become ground zero for Family Drama Central.

The Freedom Wishlist: Reclaiming Your Emotional Real Estate

This isn't surrender. This is strategic resistance. Your freedom hour isn't a suggestion—it's a non-negotiable constitutional amendment of personal sanity.

- Establish those clear boundaries we've been going on about throughout.

- Communicate without declaring war. "I love you, but I also love my uninterrupted coffee time" becomes your new mantra. Firm. Kind. Unapologetic.

- And, remember: You're not a doormat. You're a human with needs.

- Those passions you shelved during decades of parenting? Time for a comeback tour. Painting. Gardening. Competitive bird watching. Whatever makes you happy and lose track of time.

- One glorious hour. Zero interruptions. Complete and total personal sovereignty. Think of it like diplomatic immunity for your sanity.

- Of course, top up on that sense of humor (industrial strength).

You need to reframe the narrative. This isn't about pushing them away. It's about creating a healthy space. You're not being selfish. You're being human.

Some days, freedom looks like a locked bathroom door. On other days, it's a spontaneous coffee date with yourself. Celebrate those moments. Your home isn't a prison. It's a dynamic, evolving emotional landscape. Rigid expectations are emotional quicksand. The more you struggle, the deeper you sink. Adapt. Breathe. Laugh.

So, start with one item per week. Non-negotiable. Whether it's a bubble bath without interruptions or learning underwater basket weaving with toothpicks—do something purely, deliciously for you.

This isn't just survival. This is radical self-love in the face of total personal space invasion. You're not losing freedom. You're redefining it.

The Problem With Keeping Everyone Happy

While the family is busy having their dramatic life episodes, you're backstage, juggling feelings like a circus performer. One sibling argument? No problem. Two conflicting schedules? You're on it. Passive-aggressive tension brewing? Time to deploy the family peace-keeping missile.

But here's a revolutionary concept for you: You're not responsible for solving everyone's emotional puzzles.

That dynamic tension? It's not a problem. It's called growth. Healthy families have conflict. Healthy parents know when to step back. Think of yourself like a smartphone battery constantly draining from background apps. Every time you mediate, negotiate or smooth over a situation, you're spending precious emotional currency. And guess what? That account has a limit!

So what do you do?

Well, you start delegating. When Sibling A has a beef with Sibling B, your new response? "Have you talked to each other about this?" Boom. Instant emotional boundary. You're not avoiding support—you're encouraging direct communication. And the major winner here is that you are sidestepping triangulation. You see, triangulation is like emotional quicksand. The more you struggle, the deeper you sink. Your adult children are grown humans capable of resolving their own conflicts.

Your job? Cheerleader, not referee.

Reflection Exercise: The Backstage Pass to Your Emotional Management

Pull back the curtain on your peacekeeper performance. Where are you over-functioning? Where are you rescuing instead of supporting?

Scenario	What Did You Do?	How Did It Make You Feel?	Better Alternative Action	Notes/ Reflections
Example: Your child calls you to solve an argument with their sibling.	Jumped in, mediated the conversation, and solved the issue for them.	Drained and frustrated; felt like it wasn't your role.	Encourage them to communicate directly and resolve it themselves.	Reflect on how empowering them might lead to better long-term outcomes.
A family member shares an emotional problem, expecting you to fix it.				
Your adult child blames you for a personal mistake they made.				

Scenario	What Did You Do?	How Did It Make You Feel?	Better Alternative Action	Notes/ Reflections
Someone repeatedly interrupts your downtime with non-urgent requests.				

Here are a couple of pro tips for boundary mastering:

- Listen without solving

- Validate feelings without taking ownership

- Encourage direct communication

- Maintain your emotional energy reserves

Stepping back isn't abandonment. It's trust. Trust in their ability to navigate complex emotions. Trust in their capacity to resolve conflicts. Some days, supporting means doing absolutely nothing. Let that sink in.

The Emotional Energy Bank

Think of your emotional resources like a financial portfolio. Every unnecessary intervention is a withdrawal. Every boundary is a deposit.

Sure, some conflicts are necessary. Some tensions create space for understanding. Your job isn't to eliminate all friction. Your job is to create an environment where friction can exist without destruction. Healthy families aren't conflict-free. They're conflict-navigating. And by stepping back, you're teaching something profound. You're showing them how to be autonomous, how to communicate, and how to resolve conflict without constant parental mediation, plus you're making a healthy boundary deposit.

This isn't about being less loving. This is about being more strategically supportive. You're a growth facilitator. An emotional landscape architect.

Dealing With Guilt

And, there you are, sipping coffee, contemplating life, when guilt comes crashing through the door. Sound familiar? Yup. It's the guilt carousel—where every spin makes you question your parenting choices.

But before you choke on a sip of that coffee, you need to reframe guilt.

Guilt is like that annoying U-turn enthusiast that keeps rerouting you when you're pretty sure you know the way. But what if—stick with me here—guilt is actually your internal reroute oracle system trying to help you plot a healthier course?

Parents often treat guilt like a four-letter word. "Am I being a terrible parent?" "Should I be doing more?" Newsflash: You're not failing. You're recalibrating. Stop with the self-interrogation.• Setting boundaries isn't about building walls, remember? It's about creating a sustainable relationship where everyone gets to breathe.

Think of self-care as your personal pit stop. NASCAR drivers don't win races by running on fumes, and neither do parents.

Let's get complicated while we are at it. Psychologically speaking, guilt isn't the villain; it's more like that overzealous friend who wants to "help" but doesn't know how to chill. It shows up because you care—about doing better, being better, and showing up for the people you love. But guilt is a terrible project manager. Left unchecked, it turns into shame and self-doubt, derailing your confidence. A darn thorn in the side.

The trick?

See guilt for what it is: a signal, not a sentence. It's a nudge to assess your choices and values—not an invitation to throw yourself into a spiral of self-blame, despair, and execution.

Guilt, when handled right, can actually be a motivator for growth and positive change.

Here's the magic: By addressing guilt head-on, you're teaching your brain to process emotions constructively. It's emotional strength training, and guess what? The kids are watching. They're *always* watching. Scary? Right!

When they see you acknowledge, process, and reframe guilt, they learn resilience and emotional intelligence.

The Guilt Journal: Your Emotional Workout

Consider this your emotional fitness plan. "Positive Guilt Journaling" isn't some touchy-feely exercise—it's strategic self-reflection.

Think of journaling as guilt's kryptonite. When guilt hits, your mind tends to catastrophize, painting worst-case scenarios in high-def. Journaling gives you the tools to hit pause, rewind, and see the situation for what it really is:

- It gives guilt a container
- It offers perspective
- It rewires your brain

Here's how it works:

1. Catch those guilt gremlins in real-time

2. Document the moment

3. Immediately challenge the narrative

4. Reframe with radical honesty

5. **Example:**

    a. **Guilt trigger:** Told my 25-year-old son he needs to pay rent if he's living at home.

    b. **Guilt whispers:** "I'm the worst parent ever. What kind of monster charges their kid rent?"

    c. **Reframe:** "I'm teaching financial responsibility. Real-world skills don't develop in a vacuum. Paying rent means learning budgeting, understanding value, and preparing for independent living."

Guilt, when processed healthily, isn't a punishment—it's a development tool. It signals that you care deeply and want to make responsible choices.

The key?

Transform guilt from a paralyzing emotion into an actionable insight. Instead of drowning in "Am I being selfish?" ask the power question: "Am I modeling healthy boundaries for my kids?"

Answer the questions that pop into your head, of course, but reframe them instead of breaking yourself down. Start small (it's never too late for baby steps). Maybe it's reclaiming the kitchen after dinner. Perhaps it's establishing "quiet hours" or designating specific shared spaces. Each tiny boundary is a victory lap in the parenting marathon. I know, I know, we keep hammering on about boundaries—because without boundaries, your home becomes an all-you-can-eat buffet of your patience and sanity. And, guess who's doing the dishes?

Frankly, boundaries are the glue holding your "I love my family, but I also need to breathe" mantra together.

Remember, you're not just a parent—you're a relationship architect. Your job isn't to be perpetually available; it's to create a dynamic where everyone grows, respects each other's space, and occasionally shares a laugh about the whole messy, beautiful process.

Guilt doesn't get to be your copilot anymore. You're driving this family bus, and sometimes that means taking the scenic route of self-care, boundary-setting, and unapologetic personal growth.

Accepting Your Limitations

Breaking news: You are *not* actually a superhero or a professional fixer. Yup. Shocking, right? Those cape fantasies where you solve every problem, cook every meal, and emotionally rescue your adult children? Time to file that under "fiction."

Limitation acceptance isn't a weakness—it's the ultimate parental power move. Think of it like setting your smartphone battery to low-power mode. You're not broken; you're strategically conserving energy.

Now, let's deconstruct the cultural myth that parents must be omnipresent emotional vending machines. Heck, that model leads straight to Burnout City, population: you.

Numero uno... *you*!

Your adult children don't need a 24/7 crisis hotline. They need a balanced relationship where boundaries aren't just respected—they're celebrated. Every time you say "no," you're actually saying "yes" to your own mental health. Yes, yes, yes!

The Jar of No: Your Boundary Collection

Enter the "Jar of No"—part psychological intervention, part rebellious act of self-preservation. Here's how it works:

1. Grab a jar (bonus points for something decorative)

2. Write down scenarios where you typically overextend

3. Commit to releasing one "no" per week

4. Watch your personal sovereignty grow

5. **Potential "no" candidates:**

    a. Last-minute babysitting requests

    b. Endless financial bailouts

    c. Solving problems that they can handle

    d. Unsolicited advice marathons

Your exhausted brain already knows: Constant caretaking isn't sustainable. It's like trying to pour from an empty pitcher—eventually, you're just making a mess out of nothing. Not exactly what we'll refer to as constructive, realistically.

Healthy parents create healthy boundaries. Read this again and write it down!

Your limitations aren't a character flaw; they're a sign of mutual respect. Saying "no" is a skill. Like any muscle, it gets stronger with practice—plus it's a complete sentence. Start small:

- "I can't drop everything right now."
- "I'm not available this weekend."
- "That doesn't work for me."

Complete sentences. No apologetic stammering required.

Heck yes, expect some pushback. You're working with a human, even if they might seem alien at times. So, yes, your adult children might initially react like toddlers denied a cookie. Breathe. Stay consistent. They're testing the new relationship terrain. Your job isn't perpetual rescue. It's gradual guidance. Think less firefighter, more lighthouse—illuminating possibilities without jumping into every emotional storm.

So, drop the cape, pick up your boundaries, and enjoy the view.

You're Not Perfect, and That's Okay!

Perfection is a myth. It's the participation trophy of parenting that nobody actually wins. As a matter of fact, not just parenting, but life in general. It's elusive—like a unicorn or that pot of gold at the end of the rainbow.

In the real world, parenting looks less like a Pinterest board and more like a comedic disaster film. Life, reality, is not a perpetual highlight reel.

Here's another radical concept for you: Your kids don't need a flawless parent. They need a human. Someone who shows up, messes up, and keeps showing up. Those "oops" moments? They're not failures. They're master classes in real-life adulting. They don't need you on a flawless pedestal, they need you to be relatable.

Imagine you're giving a presentation and totally bomb a slide. Do you melt into a puddle of shame? Nope. You recover, crack a joke, and move on. Parenting is exactly the same. Kids learn more from how you handle mistakes than from never making them. Remember; monkey see, monkey do.

Your imperfections are teaching resilience, adaptability, and human authenticity. When you err, because we all do, just:

- own your mess
- apologize genuinely
- show them how adults take responsibility
- laugh about it (seriously)

Think of imperfect parenting as emotional cross-training. You're not dropping the ball—you're teaching your kids how to pick it up and keep playing.

When you embrace imperfection, you're doing more than surviving parenthood. You're revolutionizing it. You're showing your adult children that growth isn't about being flawless. It's about being fearlessly, magnificently human.

The best parents aren't perfect. They're present. They're real. They're willing to look ridiculous occasionally.

- Missed a call? Send a text.
- Forgot an important date? Make it up with genuine effort.
- Said something wrong? Admit it, learn from it, move forward.

And, while we're at it, avoid the following to be perfectly imperfect:

- apologizing
- hiding your mistakes
- taking yourself too seriously
- dwelling on failures
- obsessing over flaws
- doubling down on errors
- letting guilt paralyze you
- ignoring or minimizing causing hurt
- striving for impossible standards

Your imperfections aren't a weakness. They transform you from a distant, untouchable figure into a relatable, authentic human being.

Who Is Your Support Network?

Breaking news: You are not a lone wolf in this adult-child wilderness. Repeat after me: Isolation is the enemy; connection is your superpower. You are part of "the village people" (and no, not that band).

Immediately forget the lone ranger approach. Modern parenting isn't a solo sport—it's a team marathon. Your support network isn't just a luxury; it's your emotional oxygen tank. Imagine trying to assemble IKEA furniture alone. Nightmare, right? Parenting adult children is exponentially more complex. You need a crew—people who get the crazy, who'll listen without judgment, who'll offer a virtual high-five.

So, who makes the cut? Look for:

- friends who've survived similar parenting trenches
- family members who offer perspective, not criticism
- professionals who understand modern family dynamics
- online communities where raw honesty is the currency
- **Identify your ride-or-die support trio:**
    - The Emotional Dumping Ground
    - The Practical Problem Solver
    - The Perspective Shifter

These aren't just contacts. They're your personal emotional support team. And we all need a solid crew like this.

Support groups aren't group therapy—they're reality check stations. Where else can you swap stories about adult children who mysteriously forget how laundry works or how financial responsibility exists?

Online platforms offer incredible connections. Facebook groups, Reddit communities, and specialized forums—they're your 24/7 parenting emergency room. Shared experiences reduce stress, normalize challenges, and provide practical strategies. You're not just sharing—you're collectively problem-solving. Now, for you to build up a squad like this is really not rocket science. Explore:

- local parent meetups
- church groups
- community centers
- specialized online forums
- professional networking groups

Asking for help is strategic emotional intelligence. You're modeling healthy relationship dynamics for your adult children. But not all support is created equal. Thus, avoid:

- perpetual complaint circles
- judgment-heavy environments
- competitive parenting spaces

Build a support network that's part cheerleading squad, part strategic think tank, part comedy club, because parenting adult children requires humor and perspective.

Enjoy Your Retirement

Forget that outdated script where parents become background characters. Retirement isn't a waiting room. You're not on pause—you're hitting the reset button on personal joy.

Retirement isn't about killing time. It's about living it spectacularly.

Your "retirement fantasy" isn't a dusty dream. It's an actionable mission. Travel? Learn salsa dancing? Write that novel? Consider this your official permission slip.

The Monthly Passion Passport

Introducing the "Mini-Retirement Day"—your monthly passport to unapologetic self-indulgence. One day. Pure, unfiltered *you* time.

Potential adventures may include:

- watercolor painting without interruption
- a spontaneous road trip
- marathon reading without guilt
- trying that ridiculous cooking class
- binge-watching without explanations

Personal fulfillment isn't selfish. It's essential. When you invest in yourself, you're modeling healthy life design for your adult children.

Your retirement isn't about waiting. It's about creating. Start small:

- Schedule non-negotiable personal time.
- Invest in learning something wild.
- Reconnect with dormant passions.
- Explore new territories of curiosity.

Your adult children are watching. They're learning that life isn't a linear path of sacrifice. It's a dynamic, ever-evolving adventure of personal growth.

You're not just retiring. You're relaunching.

Simple Self-Care Habits: Because You're Worth It

Your body isn't just a vehicle shuttling stress from one deadline to the next. It's the motherboard of your sanity. Neglect it, and you're cruising toward burnout on a fast train fueled by exhaustion.

Carving out "me time" may feel as impossible as folding a fitted sheet. That's why self-care doesn't need to be elaborate; it needs to be sustainable. Ten-minute yoga isn't just exercise—it's a rebellious act of self-love. Those little moments where you choose movement or mindfulness? That's you, flipping the script on chaos and reclaiming control.

Remember, self-care isn't indulgent. It's essential. Because when you prioritize yourself, you're not just surviving—you're thriving.

Self-Care Strategies

Try out one thing per day—or stretch it to every three days if that feels more manageable—and notice how even the tiniest changes can ripple through your life.

Category	Activity	Why It's Great	Your Interactive Challenge
Movement Magic	Neighborhood walks	Clears the mind, gets you moving, and earns you bonus steps.	Walk without your phone. Count cool bird sightings!
	Living room dance parties	Endorphins + silliness = mood boost.	Make a playlist and dance like nobody's watching. Share your top track.
	Stretching while waiting for coffee	Multitasking genius meets tension relief.	Pick one stretch to perfect and name it after yourself.
	Gardening as a low-key workout	Physical + therapeutic, with bonus veggies or flowers!	Snap a "before and after" of your garden zone progress.
Mindfulness Hacks	Three deep breaths before reacting	Immediate calm; great for stressful moments.	Use it before responding to a frustrating text. Score your Zen out of 10.

Category	Activity	Why It's Great	Your Interactive Challenge
Mindfulness Hacks	Gratitude journaling	Helps you focus on the positives—even tiny ones count.	Write down *one* thing today that surprised you in a good way.
	Five-minute meditation sessions	Short, sweet, and scientifically proven to reduce stress.	Try a new meditation app and rate its vibes.
Three-Good-Things Ritual	Nightly gratitude reflections	Shifts focus from what's wrong to what's right.	Share your quirkiest gratitude moment with a friend.
Psychological Armor	Set non-negotiable boundaries	Protects your time, energy, and peace of mind.	Identify one "non-negotiable" this week. Enforce it like a boss.
	Celebrate microscopic victories	Boosts morale and builds resilience.	Post a "tiny win" on social media or a group chat.

Category	Activity	Why It's Great	Your Interactive Challenge
Psychological Armor	Laugh at the absurdity	Instant mood reset.	Find and share a ridiculous meme or parenting fail.
	Release toxic guilt	Frees up emotional bandwidth for things that actually matter.	Write one toxic thought on paper, then rip it up dramatically.

Your self-care is a mic-drop moment of rebellion, proving that you're not just a parent—you're a freaking legend.

Your adult children aren't watching for perfection. They're studying how to live authentically. Every passion pursued, every boundary set, every moment of unapologetic self-love is a masterclass in adulting.

"I'm doing my best, and that's enough."

Say it. Mean it. Believe it.

This isn't just a feel-good phrase. It's your daily reminder that your worth isn't measured by your kids' success, your productivity, or societal expectations. You're writing a new narrative. Not just for yourself, but for an entire generation watching how to navigate life's complexities with grace, humor, and radical self-respect.

Be you. Be validated. Be empowered.

Conclusion:

The Couch, the Chaos, and the Unexpected Grace of Parenting Adult Children

You've survived the adult-child hurricane lecture, and let's face it—this is no small feat. Forget the outdated parenting script that says your only role is to prepare them for independence and wave goodbye at 18.

Life didn't get that memo, and neither did the economy.

Being real? You're not just a support system; you're a fully dimensional human with dreams, quirks, and life beyond "Mom" and "Dad." Take a look at that kid sprawled on your couch right now.

Are they a failure?

Nope. They're still breathing...

Are you?

Definitely not.

This isn't a tragedy—it's a remix. Life, with its unpredictable beat, has placed you both in a new chapter.

Remember when they were learning to walk, and you'd hover nearby, ready to catch them before they tumbled? Parenting adult children is exactly like that—except now the falls are financial, and emotional, and sometimes involve catastrophically bad dating choices. Your job isn't to prevent the fall. It's to help them learn how to get back up. Somewhere between their childhood bedroom and your living room, something magical happens. You stop being just a parent and start becoming... a teammate. A consultant. A slightly exasperated but unconditionally loving human who understands that adulting is harder than anyone predicted.

You're not just raising a child anymore—you're navigating an economic landscape that looks more like an obstacle course designed by a drunk urban planner.

Boundaries are your superpower. Think of them like emotional guardrails. They keep everyone safe, prevent random meltdowns, and ensure nobody loses their mind—or their leftovers. Communication becomes your secret weapon. Forget perfect conversations. Aim for honest ones. Sometimes that means admitting, "I have no earthly idea how to do this either." If you can't laugh about the fact that your retirement fund is temporarily funding Netflix and pizza, you'll cry.

What you're doing right now?

It's not babysitting an overgrown teenager. It's supporting a human being through one of the most economically challenging transitions in modern history. Sky-high rents. Student loans that could fund a small country. A job market that demands five years of experience for an entry-level position where the starting salary might generously buy a week's worth of avocado toast. Hurdles you probably didn't face when you were their age.

So no, your adult child isn't lazy. They're adapting. Bootstraps aren't the answer when the system feels rigged; survival now demands strategy, collaboration, and sometimes a little help from mom or dad's fridge.

To the parent reading this: You are doing something extraordinary. Not because you're perfect, but because you're present. You're choosing connection over criticism. Support over shame. This isn't just parenting. This is a collaborative rescue mission. Economic turbulence has rewritten family dynamics. Gone are the days of "move out, get married, buy a house" as the standard life trajectory. This is now a choose-your-own-adventure story with plot twists that include moving back home, renegotiating boundaries, and managing Wi-Fi passwords like diplomatic treaties. It's not failure—it's adaptation.

The good news?

Your adult child will remember this time not as a low point, but as a period of connection and growth. They'll look back and see a parent who didn't just provide a roof but also understanding, compassion, and respect. Success isn't about them moving out by a certain age. It's about creating a bond that weathers personal growth, economic challenges, and yes, the occasional passive-aggressive standoff about dirty dishes.

You're rewriting the family playbook. Vulnerability is your strength. Asking for help, setting boundaries, and practicing radical acceptance are the hallmarks of a healthy relationship—not weaknesses. What you're doing isn't just surviving; it's creating a relationship that's resilient, honest, and occasionally laugh-out-loud funny.

And let's talk about humor—it's your survival tool. Acknowledge the chaos, but don't be afraid to laugh at it. The absurdity of life is what makes it bearable. That time they borrowed your car and left the gas tank empty? One day, it'll be a funny story. (Okay, maybe not yet, but give it time.)

Consider this: Every generation faces its unique challenges. Your parents might have had trouble imagining the family dynamics you're navigating now, and someday your adult child will marvel at how you managed to balance love, boundaries, and the occasional impromptu therapy session disguised as a late-night chat over pizza.

Yes, this chapter will end eventually. But your story together? It keeps going.

I want to hear about your story—the real, unfiltered version. Not the Instagram-perfect highlights but the messy, unpredictable, "I-can't-believe-this-is-my-life" moments. Drop me a review. Tell me what resonated, what made you laugh, what hit too close to home. Your story matters. Your struggle is valid. And your love? It's transformative.

As for that adult child on your couch? They're going to be okay. Because they have you—the parent who shows up, sometimes imperfectly, but always with love.

And hey, buy them groceries once in a while. But seriously, hide the good snacks. Some boundaries are sacred. With all the humor, hope, and caffeine-fueled solidarity in the world, know this: tough times feel long, but great stories last forever.

And, most importantly, there's profit in all labor, and every moment you invest now is shaping a future that's stronger, closer, and full of love for tomorrow and every other day that follows.

Our children are on loan to us, so make the most of what you're granted. You never raised a child, you raised an adult.

References

A guide to self-care for parents: Why making time for yourself matters. (2020). Waterford.org. https://www.waterford.org/blog/self-care-for-parents/

Acharya, U. (2024, January 12). *Reframing resistance in children and youth.* Vermont Child Welfare Training Partnership. https://vermontcwtp.org/reframing-resistance-in-children-and-youth/

Alice69. (2021, June 9). *How to reset your relationship.* Medium. https://medium.com/@alice69/how-to-reset-your-relationship-804fbcfd8835

Amy Marschall. (2023, May 15). *6 de-escalation techniques to diffuse conflict.* Verywell Mind. https://www.verywellmind.com/deescalation-techniques-to-diffuse-conflict-7498049

Arntz, A. (2005). *Pathological dependency: Distinguishing functional from emotional dependency.* American Psychological Association. https://psycnet.apa.org/record/2005-14118-007

Article 8: Respect for your private and family life. (2021, June 24). Equality and Human Rights Commission. https://www.equalityhumanrights.com/human-rights/human-rights-act/article-8-respect-your-private-and-family-life

Ayeni-Bepo, A. (n.d.). *Methods to deal with an adult narcissistic child.* Overcomers Counseling. https://overcomewithus.com/narcissist-personality/methods-to-deal-with-an-adult-narcissistic-child

Behere, A. P., Basnet, P., & Campbell, P. (2017). Effects of family structure on mental health of children: A preliminary study. *Indian Journal of Psychological Medicine, 39*(4), 457–463. https://doi.org/10.4103/0253-7176.211767

Bernstein, J. (2015, September 7). *Creating boundaries with dependent adult children.* Psychology Today. https://www.psychologytoday.com/intl/blog/liking-the-child-you-love/201509/creating-boundaries-dependent-adult-children

Bernstein, J. (2023a, July 17). *Setting win-win boundaries with your adult child.* Psychology Today. https://www.psychologytoday.com/intl/blog/liking-the-child-you-love/202307/setting-win-win-boundaries-with-your-adult-child

Bernstein, J. (2023b, October 7). *How to keep an adult child from walking all over you.* Psychology Today. https://www.psychologytoday.com/intl/blog/liking-the-child-you-love/202310/stop-letting-your-adult-child-walk-all-over-you

Bernstein, J. (2024a, January 7). *When your partner doesn't grasp your adult child's struggles.* Psychology Today. https://www.psychologytoday.com/intl/blog/liking-the-child-you-love/202401/when-your-partner-doesnt-grasp-your-adult-childs-struggles

Bernstein, J. (2024b, October 6). *Helping your adult child with finances without enabling.* Psychology Today. https://www.psychologytoday.com/intl/blog/liking-the-child-you-love/202410/helping-your-adult-child-with-finances-without-enabling

Bernstein, L. (2015, October 27). *What not to say to your adult child after a breakup.* Next Avenue. https://www.nextavenue.org/what-not-to-say-to-your-heartbroken-child/

Bethesda Senior Living Community. (2024, May 14). *9 tips for improving relationships with your adult children.* LifeStream at Youngtown. https://www.lifestreamatyoungtown.com/blog/9-tips-for-improving-relationships-with-your-adult-children

BetterHelp Editorial Team. (2024a, October 12). *What is tough love? Setting boundaries with compassion.* BetterHelp. https://www.betterhelp.com/advice/love/what-you-need-to-know-about-tough-love/

BetterHelp Editorial Team. (2024b, October 16). *The importance of setting boundaries for your mental health and safety.* BetterHelp. https://www.betterhelp.com/advice/general/the-importance-of-setting-boundaries-10-benefits-for-you-and-your-relationships/

Communicating boundaries. (n.d.). Cerebral. https://cerebral.com/care-resources/communicating-boundaries

Cook, A. (n.d.). *How to replenish your emotional bank account.* Dr. Alison Cook. https://www.dralisoncook.com/blog/how-to-replenish-your-emotional-bank-account

Creating safe spaces for courageous conversations. (n.d.). Sage Thinking. https://www.sagethinking.com.au/resources/articles/on-leadership/creating-safe-spaces-for-courageous-conversations/

Crossfield, A. (2020, June 25). *Why does my teen procrastinate?* Psychology Today. https://www.psychologytoday.com/intl/blog/emotionally-healthy-teens/202006/why-does-my-teen-procrastinate

Cuncic, A. (2024, February 12). *7 active listening techniques for better communication.* Verywell Mind. https://www.verywellmind.com/what-is-active-listening-3024343

Daugherty, G. (2023, July 18). *Managing your money after you retire.* Investopedia. https://www.investopedia.com/articles/retirement/05/managingincome.asp

Dealing with a grown child who is unemployed and living at home. (n.d.). Focus on the Family. https://www.focusonthefamily.com/family-qa/dealing-with-a-grown-child-who-is-unemployed-and-living-at-home/

Degges-White, S. (2014, October 11). *7 tips for mothers of adult addicts.* Psychology Today. https://www.psychologytoday.com/intl/blog/lifetime-connections/201410/7-tips-for-mothers-of-adult-addicts

Dooba, I. (2023, December 24). *No such thing as constructive criticism.* Medium. https://medium.com/@IbraheemDooba/no-such-thing-as-constructive-criticism-c2e91e67bd3e

Drake, K. (2022, March 25). *How to deal with guilt so it doesn't drag you down.* Psych Central. https://psychcentral.com/health/tips-for-dealing-with-guilt

Epstein, S. (2023, September 26). *1 sure way to improve relationships with adult children.* Psychology Today. https://www.psychologytoday.com/intl/blog/between-the-generations/202309/1-sure-way-to-improve-relationships-with-adult-children

Fairbank, R. (2024, April 1). *Estrangement is never easy or straightforward. Psychologists can help.* American Psychological Association. https://www.apa.org/monitor/2024/04/healing-pain-estrangement

5 Steps to help neurodivergent young adults build relationships. (n.d.). Parents Helping Parents. https://www.php.com/elearning/neurodiverse-adults-building-relationships/

Fletcher, J. (2016, May 17). *How to deal when you don't approve of your adult kids' relationship.* Psych Central. https://psychcentral.com/lib/when-you-dont-approve-of-your-adult-childs-relationship

Fry, R., Passel, J. S., & Cohn, D. (2020, September 4). *A majority of young adults in the U.S. live with their parents for the first time since the Great Depression.* Pew Research Center. https://www.pewresearch.org/short-reads/2020/09/04/a-majority-of-young-adults-in-the-u-s-live-with-their-parents-for-the-first-time-since-the-great-depression/

Gallo, A. (2024a, January 2). *What is active listening?* Harvard Business Review. https://hbr.org/2024/01/what-is-active-listening

Gallo, A. (2024b, October 21). *How to master conflict resolution.* Harvard Business Review. https://hbr.org/2024/10/how-to-master-conflict-resolution

Gillette, H. (2016, July 12). *7 de-escalation techniques to consider during conflict.* Psych Central. https://psychcentral.com/health/tips-for-de-escalating-an-argument

Guarnotta, E. (2024, July 16). *Guide for parents: Helping your child with alcoholism or drug abuse.* Greenhouse Treatment Center. https://greenhousetreatment.com/family-resources/helping-your-child/

Gupta, C. (2021, July 21). *What accepting your limitations looks like.* Medium. https://medium.com/the-ascent/what-accepting-your-limitations-looks-like-a39a4df368fe

Gupta, S. (2024, April 28). *How to thrive as a blended family.* Verywell Mind. https://www.verywellmind.com/blended-family-8637072

Hammond, C. (2018, August 31). *10 strategies for coping with an adult narcissistic child*. Psych Central. https://psychcentral.com/pro/exhausted-woman/2018/08/10-strategies-for-coping-with-an-adult-narcissistic-child

Health, M. V. (2017, February 16). *How to set expectations for adult children living at home*. My Vanderbilt Health. https://my.vanderbilthealth.com/adult-children-living-at-home/

Heitler, S. (2012, May 8). *Skip the criticism altogether. Give feedback instead*. Psychology Today. https://www.psychologytoday.com/intl/blog/resolution-not-conflict/201205/skip-the-criticism-altogether-give-feedback-instead

Henley, D. (2024, August 22). *How to make friends with your adult children*. Thrive Global. https://community.thriveglobal.com/how-to-make-friends-with-your-adult-children/

How parents can help adult children living at home. (2024, July 10). Bank of America Private Bank. https://www.privatebank.bankofamerica.com/articles/adult-children-living-with-parents.html

How to have meaningful conversations with your adult kids. (2022, September 28). Empty Nest Blessed. https://emptynestblessed.com/2022/09/28/meaningful-conversations-adult-kids/

How to navigate your transition from child to caregiver. (2024, January 17). National Church Residences. https://www.nationalchurchresidences.org/blog/how-to-navigate-your-transition-from-child-to-caregiver/

How to start over in a relationship. (2022, August 15). Anchor Light Therapy Collective. https://anchorlighttherapy.com/how-to-start-over-in-a-relationship/

How to support your LGBTQ child. (n.d.). HealthPartners. https://www.healthpartners.com/blog/how-to-support-your-lgbtq-child/

How to use "I" statements instead of "You" statements during difficult conversations. (2024, March 4). Relationships Australia. https://www.relationshipsnsw.org.au/blog/i-statements-vs-you-statements/

Jacobs, M. (2022, October 10). *Living with grandchildren: A survival guide.* Nu?Detroit. https://www.nu-detroit.com/surviving-grandchildren/

Kate. (2020, June 29). *Supporting a young person when they come out.* YoungMinds. https://www.youngminds.org.uk/parent/blog/supporting-a-young-person-when-they-come-out/

King, D. (2022, June 19). *Are you assuming your kids will be your caregivers?* Johnson McGinnis. https://www.tn-elderlaw.com/post/are-you-assuming-your-kids-will-be-your-caregivers

Kinzler, P. (n.d.). *Retirement 101: A beginner's guide to retirement.* Trinity College. https://legacy.trincoll.edu/retirement

Lander, L., Howsare, J., & Byrne, M. (2013). The impact of substance use disorders on families and children: From theory to practice. *Social Work in Public Health, 28*(3-4), 194–205. https://doi.org/10.1080/19371918.2013.759005

Lawrence, P. (1969, January). *How to deal with resistance to change.* Harvard Business Review. https://hbr.org/1969/01/how-to-deal-with-resistance-to-change

Lee, C. I. (2022, May 9). *How to help your child overcome unemployment depression.* LA Concierge Psychologist. https://laconciergepsychologist.com/blog/overcome-unemployment-depression/

Living close to your grandkids: How much space? (2023, February 14). GrandkidsMatter. https://grandkidsmatter.org/hot-topics/healthy-relationships/living-close-to-your-grandkids-how-much-space/

MacNamara, D. (2024). *The surprising secret behind kids' resistance and opposition.* Neufeldinstitute. https://neufeldinstitute.org/editorials/the-surprising-secret-behind-kids-resistance-and-opposition/

Managing stress. (n.d.). CDC Mental Health. https://www.cdc.gov/mental-health/living-with/index.html

Matthews, J. (2023, August 30). *Support for parents: why it's important and where to get it.* Raising Children Network. https://raisingchildren.net.au/grown-ups/services-support/about-services-support/support-for-parents-why-its-important

McCoy, K. (2021, February 25). *Living with estrangement.* Psychology Today. https://www.psychologytoday.com/intl/blog/complicated-love/202102/living-with-estrangement

Moore, M. (2022, September 8). *The importance of personal boundaries.* Psych Central. https://psychcentral.com/relationships/the-importance-of-personal-boundaries

Nash, J. (2018, January 5). *How to set healthy boundaries & build positive relationships.* Positive Psychology. https://positivepsychology.com/great-self-care-setting-healthy-boundaries/

Odell, C. A. (n.d.). *How is life tree(ting) you?: Trust, safety, and respect - the importance of boundaries | student affairs.* Stanford University. https://studentaffairs.stanford.edu/how-life-treeting-you-importance-of-boundaries

Orford, S. (2023, June 28). *How to manage when your adult children are living at home.* Healthline. https://www.healthline.com/health/how-to-manage-when-your-adult-children-are-living-at-home

Pastore, S. (n.d.). *Dealing with divorce and your adult child*. Mainline Family Divorce Center. https://www.mainlinedivorcemediator.com/healthy-divorce-blog/bid/302320/dealing-with-divorce-and-your-adult-child

Pattemore, C. (2021, June 3). *10 ways to build and preserve better boundaries*. Psych Central. https://psychcentral.com/lib/10-way-to-build-and-preserve-better-boundaries

Peterson, J. (2022, April 11). *Learn the secrets to surviving your adult children's love relationships*. The Oakland Press. https://www.theoaklandpress.com/2022/04/11/learn-the-secrets-to-surviving-your-adult-childrens-love-relationships/

Pikiewicz, K. (2015, April 24). *How trying to make everyone happy can make you miserable*. Psychology Today. https://www.psychologytoday.com/intl/blog/meaningful-you/201504/how-trying-to-make-everyone-happy-can-make-you-miserable

Pincus, D. (n.d.). *Adult children living at home: 9 rules to help you maintain sanity*. Empowering Parents. https://www.empoweringparents.com/article/adult-children-living-at-home-part-ii-9-rules-to-help-you-maintain-sanity/

Privacy, monitoring and trust: the teenage years. (2024, March 7). Raising Children Network. https://raisingchildren.net.au/pre-teens/communicating-relationships/family-relationships/privacy-trust-teen-years

Pugle, M. (2023, March 27). *What is the difference between supporting and enabling?* Psych Central. https://psychcentral.com/health/what-is-the-difference-between-supporting-and-enabling

Ragland, L. (2023, September 12). *Ways to manage stress.* WebMD. https://www.webmd.com/balance/stress-management/stress-management

Rand Caponey, R. (n.d.). *Responding in love to an adult gay child.* Focus on the Family. https://www.focusonthefamily.com/parenting/responding-in-love-to-an-adult-gay-child/

Raypole, C. (2020, March 31). *Repressed emotions: Finding and releasing them.* Healthline. https://www.healthline.com/health/repressed-emotions

Raypole, C. (2024, January 26). *Guilt makes a heavy burden. Don't let it drag you down.* Healthline. https://www.healthline.com/health/mental-health/how-to-stop-feeling-guilty

Rochman, J. (2022, October 31). *The unique joys and challenges of parenting a neurodivergent young adult.* Advance LA. https://www.advancela.org/the-unique-joys-and-challenges-of-parenting-a-neurodivergent-young-adult/

Sahadi, J. (2024, January 25). *A lot of parents still help support adult children between the ages of 18 and 34.* CNN. https://www.cnn.com/2024/01/25/success/parenting-adult-children-living-home/index.html

Salathe, S. R. (2024, August 16). *How to redefine your relationship with your kids as an empty nester.* Flow Space. https://www.theflowspace.com/interpersonal-health/family/redefining-your-relationship-kids-empty-nest-2951212/

Saline, S. (2021, November 3). *Productive procrastination and ADHD: How to stop running in place and start tackling your goals.* Dr. Sharon Saline. https://drsharonsaline.com/productive-procrastination-and-adhd-how-to-stop-running-in-place-and-start-tackling-your-goals/

Sanok, J. (2022, April 14). *A guide to setting better boundaries.* Harvard Business Review. https://hbr.org/2022/04/a-guide-to-setting-better-boundaries

Schwartz, D. (2021, July 13). *The importance of self-care for parents.* Psychology Today. https://www.psychologytoday.com/intl/blog/adolescents-explained/202107/the-importance-of-self-care-for-parents

Scott, E. (2024, March 6). *Family conflict resolution tips and strategies.* Verywell Mind. https://www.verywellmind.com/family-conflict-resolution-solutions-3144540

Segal, J., & Robinson, L. (2024, February 5). *Blended family and step-parenting tips.* HelpGuide. https://www.helpguide.org/family/parenting/step-parenting-blended-families

Seither, M. (n.d.). *Don't let your expectations push away your adult children.* Focus on the Family Canada. https://www.focusonthefamily.ca/content/dont-let-your-expectations-push-away-your-adult-children

Self-care for parents: Tips & advice. (n.d.). Child Mind Institute. https://childmind.org/article/self-care-for-parents-tips-advice/

Seltzer, L. F. (2017, July 11). *Yes, you can't!—Why you should affirm your limitations.* Psychology Today. https://www.psychologytoday.com/intl/blog/evolution-the-self/201707/yes-you-can-t-why-you-should-affirm-your-limitations

Shetty, A. (2023). How intergenerational housing can help solve Toronto's housing crisis — and allow seniors to age in place. In *CBC*. https://www.cbc.ca/news/canada/kitchener-waterloo/living-at-home-multigenerational-parents-adult-children-1.6965979

Singletary, M. (2024, February 14). *When it's time to financially cut off your adult children.* The Washington Post. https://www.washingtonpost.com/business/2024/02/14/financial-cut-off-adult-children/

Steinberg, L. (2023). *Speaking of psychology: How parents and their adult children can build strong relationships, with Laurence Steinberg, PhD.* American Psychological Association. https://www.apa.org/news/podcasts/speaking-of-psychology/parent-adult-children-relationships

Stoltzfus, J. (2020, June 22). *To fund or not to fund your young adult child. That is the question!* Parents Letting Go. https://parentslettinggo.com/to-fund-or-not-to-fund-your-young-adult-child-that-is-the-question/

Streep, P. (2024, January 18). *Why parents and adult children must maintain boundaries.* Psychology Today. https://www.psychologytoday.com/intl/blog/tech-support/202401/adult-children-parents-and-the-issue-of-boundaries

Tahmincioglu, E. (2007, June 3). *Tough love can help that grown child get a job.* NBC News. https://www.nbcnews.com/id/wbna18926704

Tang, F. (2024, January 11). *Why tough love works when we need to change behaviours.* Medium. https://medium.com/the-happy-teachers-series/why-tough-love-works-when-we-need-to-change-behaviours-fcf568b6e535

10 ways to practice self-care as a parent. (2024, May 21). Cleveland Clinic. https://health.clevelandclinic.org/realistic-ways-to-practice-self-care-as-a-parent

The importance of "I-Statements" in relationships. (n.d.). Tony Robbins. Retrieved November 28, 2024, from https://www.tonyrobbins.com/blog/words-matter-you-vs-i?srsltid=AfmBOoo61cpTJ7BS00YT4QaxMw_UGbeU1LXMjws7ENf_gbE_kns0VNWE

Top causes of relationship strain and coping techniques. (n.d.). Veritas Psychotherapy. https://veritaspsychotherapy.ca/blog/relationship-strain-and-coping-techniques/

Trueblood, A. R. (2023, July 20). *5 strategies to raise your emotional bank account.* Psychology Today. https://www.psychologytoday.com/intl/blog/emotional-self-care/202307/5-strategies-to-raise-your-emotional-bank-account

Van Loon, L. M. A., Van de Ven, M. O. M., Van Doesum, K. T. M., Witteman, C. L. M., & Hosman, C. M. H. (2013). The relation between parental mental illness and adolescent mental health: The role of family factors. *Journal of Child and Family Studies, 23*(7), 1201–1214. https://doi.org/10.1007/s10826-013-9781-7

Wein, H. (2021, April). *Good sleep for good health.* NIH News in Health; National Institutes of Health. https://newsinhealth.nih.gov/2021/04/good-sleep-good-health

What is failure to launch syndrome in young adults? (2022, October 7). Newport Institute. https://www.newportinstitute.com/resources/co-occurring-disorders/failure-to-launch-syndrome/

When helping doesn't help: How to avoid "enabling." (2019, August 29). Dr. Susan Biali Haas. https://susanbiali.com/how-to-avoid-enabling/

Woollacott, A. (2018, March 30). *Reclaiming emotions.* Medium. https://medium.com/high-sensitivity/reclaiming-emotions-1b17e7bb959

Yellinek, A. (n.d.). *Managing your adult child who is struggling to launch.* Center for Living Well with ADHD. Retrieved November 28, 2024, from https://centerforlivingwellwithadhd.org/managing-your-adult-child-who-is-struggling-to-launch/

Made in the USA
Columbia, SC
26 February 2025